The Talking Stick

VOLUME 22

IN RETROSPECT

The Talking Stick

VOLUME 22

IN RETROSPECT

A publication of the
Jackpine Writers' Bloc

Send correspondence to Jackpine Writers' Bloc, 13320 149th Avenue,
Menahga, MN 56464. sharrick1@wcta.net.

This activity is made possible, in part, by a grant from the Region 2 Arts
Council funded by an appropriation from the Minnesota State
Legislature with money from the State's general fund.

ISBN: 978-1-928690-22-1

THE TALKING STICK

TABLE OF CONTENTS

TABLE OF CONTENTS

TABLE OF CONTENTS

TABLE OF CONTENTS

CO—EDITOR'S NOTE — SHARON HARRIS

Editor's Choice: "giving it up" by Peggy Trojan (p. 94)

It happens to me every year. When I first read the submissions, I don't completely connect with them. I have to read them at least two or three times before I find the ones that move me. I have to read, pause, and read again to get into the heart of them.

Discussing them at the Editorial Board meeting helps me clarify my thoughts. I am first and foremost a poet, and poems are always my favorite way of expressing feelings.

I found a few gems this year. Several described right where I am in life with my mother as she grows older and more feeble and forgetful. "Last Rites" by Kate Halverson (p. 192) describes something so true but it is something you hate to admit out loud. Death is approaching our elderly loved ones as we busy ourselves trying to make their last years worth living. "Bubble" by Eric Chandler (p. 142) tells me of a failed relationship. The yearning there is something I've felt before. Why does love have to change and go away?

But my favorite this year is "giving it up" by Peggy Trojan (p. 94). This poem is a heart-wrenching list of all the things a person has done in his or her life, things they enjoyed, things that made life worth living. Asking to come home. Does that mean begging to go home from the nursing home? Or going home to the afterlife? Whatever it means—it sums up a whole life—a beautiful important life and the list of all the memories along the way.

co-Editor's note – Tarah L. Wolff

Editor's Choice: "South of the K-Mart on Lake" by Kathryn Knudson (p. 170)

I chose this poem this year because I felt it was one of the best (if not the best) example of using as few words as possible to create a point. In this case I felt it was more than a point, even more than a feeling; it was a complete sensation of place, time and despair that cannot be touched or changed. What is interesting too is that this place doesn't just exist in the literal "real" world but I think this place, that she created so completely (in so few words), also exists as people as well.

Maybe we've all been there in our mental lives, in a place we don't settle into, a place we don't want to stay—ruts happen to us all. But I think some people never leave them, some people are the living room furniture that, no matter how many times you rearrange it, it still doesn't look right because it's the room too. Maybe they just never found the right room to park in—there are so many rooms it seems we need to walk through before finding the room we look right in—maybe some people never find it. I think a lot of us creative people can attest to that feeling completely; it took me years to be proud of feeling like the black sheep in my family.

This is the first year in many that we got the chance to use artwork for the cover of the book so I was excited when one of our local artists (Terri Young, look her up online!) contributed a piece for us. I've known her for years and always admired her beautiful work so playing with this year's cover, I was able to really step up and do something markedly different. So much fun!

I sure hope this year's book reaches out to you as it always does for me, whether it's a few sentences of one story or many works. Everyone in this year's book should be very proud of their words!

JUDGES

Doris Stengel, Poetry Judge

Doris Lueth Stengel, a retired schoolteacher, lives in Brainerd, Minnesota. She is past president of the League of Minnesota Poets and the National Federation of State Poetry Societies (NFSPS). She has poetry and articles published in journals, magazines, and anthologies including *Encore, Dust & Fire, The Talking Stick, Lake Country Journal, Her Voice* and *County Lines.* Her chapbook *SMALL TOWN LINES* was published by Finishing Line Press, Georgetown, Kentucky, in July 2012.

Jill Johnson, Creative Nonfiction Judge

Jill grew up in Strandquist, Minnesota, population 69, and Karlstad, Minnesota, population 760. Jill and her husband Deane documented and photographed our state's smallest incorporated cities with a population near 100. *Little Minnesota: 100 Towns Around 100* chronicles the history of each town, and highlights points of interest. In 2001, Jill opened an independent bookstore, Beagle Books, in downtown Park Rapids. Jill and Deane live north of Park Rapids on the road to Itasca State Park.

John Reimringer, Fiction Judge

John Reimringer's first novel, *Vestments*, was named a best book of 2010 by *Publishers Weekly*, was featured on Minnesota Public Radio's "Midmorning," and won the 2011 Minnesota Book Award for fiction. Born in Fargo, North Dakota, and raised in Topeka, Kansas, Reimringer teaches at Normandale Community College and lives in St. Paul's Hamline-Midway neighborhood with his wife, the poet Katrina Vandenberg, and their daughter Anna. John's website is: www.johnreimringer.com.

WINNERS

Poetry 1st Place
"Getting Stoned with Virginia Woolf" (p. 1) by Kari E. Hagstrom

Kari E. Hagstrom is a Minnesotan, born and bred. She grew up in Alexandria, Minnesota, and received a B.A. in English from the College of St. Benedict. She currently resides in Elbow Lake, Minnesota. She has had poems published in *Lake Region Review* and *Gypsy Cab*.

Creative Nonfiction 1st Place
"#55" (p. 2) by Kit Rohrbach

Kit Rohrbach's writing has been published in *Green Blade, Dust & Fire* and *Poetic Strokes*. It has been featured at the exhibitions at Crossings in Zumbrota and read by Garrison Keillor on "Prairie Home Companion." Last year her poetry won both the popular choice and critic's choice awards at the Northwoods Art & Book Festival in Hackensack. Kit is single and has four cats and enjoys living that cliche.

Fiction 1st Place
"A River Runs Through It" (p. 3) by Mike Lein

Mike Lein lives near the Twin Cities where he develops environmental protection programs. He spends time at his lake cabin with family and dogs, fishing, hunting, and writing creative non-fiction. His work has appeared in *Lake Country Journal Magazine, The Talking Stick, Cabin Life, Country,* and *The Montana Sporting Journal* and others. He frequents meetings of the Jackpine Writers' Bloc whenever possible where other members try to force him to write fiction.

2ND PLACE AND HONORABLE MENTION

Poetry 2nd Place:

Scott Daniel Boras "Early Bird" (p. 7)

Poetry Honorable Mention:

Eric Chandler "Bubble" (p. 142)
Peggy Trojan "Photograph" (p. 100)
Kate Halverson "Last Rites" (p. 192)
John Thornberg "Postcard" (p. 200)
Kristin F. Johnson "The Morning After" (p. 248)

Creative Nonfiction 2nd Place:

Dennis Herschbach "Attitude Adjustment" (p. 8)

Creative Nonfiction Honorable Mention:

Tim J. Brennan "What I Know about Alzheimer's" (p. 25)
Mike Lein "Labrador Spring" (p. 75)
Deb Nelson "The First Dress" (p. 213)

Fiction 2nd Place:

Flo Golod "The Inventory" (p. 12)

Fiction Honorable Mention:

Audrey Kletscher Helbling "The Final Chapter" (p. 19)
Adrian S. Potter "An Annotated Version of Hell" (p. 103)

The Talking Stick

VOLUME 22

IN RETROSPECT

Kari E. Hagstrom *Poetry 1st Place*

Getting Stoned with Virginia Woolf

Did the stones she chose call to her?
Sing out her essence?
Walk, stoop, heft, collect,
her pockets filling

with stones on the way to the river.
Did they simply want to be wet
their rough edges polished smooth?

I think of her sometimes, out on walks,
the stones calling to me,
stoop, collect, pocket them home.
Was hers a fierce longing
to leave? Or a distaste

for being here, the denseness
of living a corporeal life.
I think of her sometimes, my pockets filling
with stones, anchoring
me here like cats sleeping
on my chest and feet lovingly
keeping me here
like great furry stones.

Sometimes I wonder
about her sad brilliance
light flashing on moving water or
lying dormant on the bottom
like a river
stone.

Kit Rohrbach *Creative Nonfiction 1st Place*

#55

It was a small room, strung with colored cables. Intimate blue lights blinked against shadowed corners and shallow breaths. The voice from the bed came soft as pillows, white as sheets. "There's something I have to tell you."

I was standing by the window watching snowflakes, pale and cold against the evening sky. Trying to count them. How many snowflakes? How many years? I knew exactly, of course. But snowflakes are easier than years; they pass much more quickly. "It's snowing," I said.

"This is important. You need to know."

How many fallen? How many still hanging in the air? "The forecast is only for 1-3 inches. It should be easing off soon."

"Listen to me."

I was listening. I heard the wind escape around a corner of the building, as though it would rather be anywhere else. Down the block, a siren cried urgency through the cotton gauze of the snowfall. There were footsteps and voices in the hallway, and the shush of rubber-wheeled carts. I listened as the heartbeat blip smoothed to a steady hum. The snow stopped.

A nurse spoke gently from the doorway. "Would you like a few moments?"

"No."

I would have liked years, perhaps. Years that were different, the way snowflakes are different, each from the other. What if there was one drifting down toward the sidewalk that was exactly like one that fell half a century ago? Would it make a difference? If truths had been told, would the night have felt less frozen?

I left the hospital. Snow clumped and crunched beneath my boots. Halos of secrets hung like ghosts around the streetlights.

Mike Lein *Fiction 1st Place*

A River Runs Through It

The Crow Wing River is a quiet Minnesota river, flowing slowly over a smooth sand bottom, not thundering downhill over boulders like a Montana trout stream. Fifty years ago, Grandpa's cabin was barely visible to river travelers, tucked away in the woods above, only noticeable due to the short wooden dock protruding from the shore. If I remember things right, most of my childhood was spent sprawled out on that dock, the rough-sawn wood prickling the bare skin of my stomach and the sun burning my back.

The grassy weeds on the sand bottom beneath the dock waved back and forth with the rhythm of the current, periodically offering glimpses of the hiding places of crayfish, minnows, and fish. Hypnotized by the flow of the river, it was easy then to dream about jumping into the canoe and escaping down river from Nimrod—floating past Motley and Brainerd in the dark, undetected. Past the glaring lights of industrial parks of "The Cities," all the way to the freedom and novelty of the ocean. I didn't really want to escape from the cabin or dock. But it was an adventure worth dreaming about.

Just a rotted post or two of the old dock remains now, half submerged and hidden by the reeds at water's edge. But I was back now, on a new dock, with a new dream.

She hadn't said much. This was her first time in this strange place and, let's be honest, we hadn't spent much time together. She held my hand with her left, clutched her pink Barbie fishing pole with her right, and considered the river, bright brown eyes taking in the green expanse, long dark hair blowing across that perfect face.

At barely four years old, she had already experienced considerable turmoil, more than I ever had as a kid. I wondered if she was confused by life so far, or didn't even think about it. I had noticed that she didn't know what to call me. What do you call a sort of unofficial Step-grand-father? I knew one thing for sure. I really wanted her to like me.

"It's a big river, isn't it?" I said breaking the silence.

"No, it's not. It's just a little river," she replied with her usual contrariness.

"But it is," I said. "This river follows all the way down past your Grandpa's house, past your house, gets even bigger, and ends up in the ocean where the Little Mermaid and all her friends live. She could swim here if she wanted to. You might catch her with your Barbie pole."

I immediately regretted that last comment. I think I was trying too hard.

She looked at me like I was the dumbest old guy on earth. "No, I couldn't—she's too big. And Ariel doesn't eat worms!" she stated forcibly, pointing to the white Styrofoam container of "icky" night crawlers we had purchased last night in Motley.

I sat down on the smooth cool plastic decking of the new dock and tried another movie. "Let's see what does eat them. Maybe you can catch Nemo, that goofy little fish."

"No, I can't. Nemo lives in Australia."

"Well, maybe. But I've seen a turtle over there on that log that looks a lot like Nemo's pal Crunch."

"His name is Crush," she said. "And he doesn't live here either."

My knowledge of kid movies was obviously limited, dated, and starting to show. It was time to try another angle. "OK, Princess, I think you watch too many movies. Lie down on the dock and let's see what does live here."

That brought a smile. She did like the nickname I had chosen for her and never fought that. She flopped down beside me, a bit clumsy in her tight pink lifejacket, and peered down into gold sand and green weeds of the river. I kept my mouth shut and waited for a reaction.

"I don't see anything," she said after a moment. "Just grass and dirt."

"The fish are here," I insisted, "right there in the weeds. I know them by name—Red Eye is my favorite. He's a Rocker."

She looked up from the water with one more dubious look in those seriously brown eyes. "A Rocker?"

"A rock bass. I call them 'Rockers' because they look cool and have red eyes. You know, like Mick Jagger."

That got another dumb look. I quit talking, pried the lid off the bait container, and grabbed the first squirming reddish-brown crawler that was unlucky enough to be on top of the bedding.

"You have to be ready." I threaded the squirming bait onto the hot pink hook we had picked out at the bait store. "Red Eye is always hungry. I'll cast it out."

"No!" She sat up quickly, almost rolling off the side of the dock, reaching for the pole. "I've been practicing—I can do it!"

She swung the short pole back, readying the cast. The pink and white bobber attached to the line would have smacked me in the face, right between the eyes. But having spent hours on this dock with two sons during an earlier phase of my life, I was ready and ducked in time. It sailed out across the water and splashed into the slow current five feet from the dock. The bobber had hardly righted itself when a bright green shadow rose up out of the weeds and inhaled the sinking night crawler.

It was an epic battle of man or, in this case, kid versus fish. The green rock bass pulled the pink bobber under the dock and down around through the weeds, clearly visible in the clean water of the river. My little princess squealed as she cranked the reel, encumbered by the puffy foam lifejacket. I held onto the back of that lifejacket to keep her from stepping off the dock. It all came together when she jerked back on the short pole and brought the six-inch fish flying out of the water and flopping onto the dock.

I quickly pressed the flopper to the dock before it did much damage and grabbed it by a toothless lip. I gently wormed the hook out and presented it to her—half a foot of gleaming green and gold scales with dime-sized blood-red eyes.

"See why I call him Red Eye?"

"Why are his eyes all bloody?" she asked as a small finger reached out, bright pink nail polish meeting wet green scales.

"That's just the way they come—how come your dog has black eyes?"

She gave me that dumb old guy look again. "He has black fur—he's supposed to have black eyes."

"Well, OK—let's just let him go quick. Watch out, he might splash you!" She laid down on the dock, watching closely as I slid Red Eye into the water. Free again, the fish darted back down to the weeds and disappeared.

She watched the weeds waving slowly with the river's flow, dipping her fingers in the warm water, feeling the current rippling past them. I waited for her to make the next move.

She rolled over and reached up for the pole. "Paul—let's try again! I need another worm!"

I got busy, reached for a new victim from the bait container, and kept my mouth shut. At least I had a name now. This clearly was time for a little less talk and a lot more action.

Scott Daniel Boras *Poetry 2nd Place*

Early Bird

At breakfast my father
has eggs and coffee
and shrugs off
anything elaborate.
He cooks them his way,
with each yolk intact
so the whites are not runny.
And with a steel spatula
he bends a patient wrist
to flip at the hiss-pop
   crackle and bite.
By now the gurgle of
the coffeemaker announces
the resignation of heavy
grounds that will wait there
   until tomorrow.

He sits alone at the table
with a fork, plate, and mug.
And the day begins
without frustration,
without the need
for explanations beyond
these little rituals
that leave their mark
like a yellow smear
across my mother's
best dishes—
simple ceremonies of how
I always saw my father,
   unsweetened and over easy.

Dennis Herschbach *Creative Nonfiction 2nd Place*

Attitude Adjustment

I finished pronouncing those familiar words, "Earth to earth, ashes to ashes, dust to dust," followed by, "Let us depart in peace."

The mourners returned to their cars, all except for three sisters, well, half-sisters, who stood at the foot of their mother's casket, holding hands. I remained at the head of the casket, standing guard as it were, until the cemetery workers came to begin filling the hole. I watched the sisters, Nancy, Nancy, and Emily and reflected on what had transpired in the days leading up to Jean's funeral as well as during the funeral itself.

Jean, their biological mother, had lived a difficult life, pregnant as a teenager three times in three years by three different men. Before me stood the sum of her contribution to the world—three daughters.

Nancy the Elder had high cheek bones, blue eyes, and blond hair as do many people of Finnish descent. Emily wore her six-feet-three-inches of height with elegance, and her black skin was in dark contrast to that of her sisters. Nancy the Younger had naturally curly hair close-cropped to her head, and it framed her olive-skinned face. For sisters, they bore little semblance to each other.

In the days leading up to the funeral, Tony, Jean's husband and Nancy the Younger's father, had phoned Emily to tell her of Jean's death.

"I don't think it would be a good idea for you to come to the funeral. After all, Emily, you know that people would talk. I think it would be best if you stayed away." Emily was married to a man from Africa, and consequently her children were very dark skinned. She decided to ignore Tony's suggestion.

The night before the funeral, I visited with the family: Nancy, Nancy, Emily, and Tony, who was definitely not happy.

He explained to me that no one was going to show up for the funeral, and he wanted the service short and without a maudlin message. "Just get it over with," he said. "No one will want to speak, so don't invite them to do so."

After the meeting, Emily lingered so we could talk.

"Tony said he doesn't want me or my family to attend the funeral. What should I do?" she asked as tears rolled down her cheeks.

"To not come would deny your existence," I advised. "For your sake and the sake of your children, not only do I think you should be there, I think you must attend."

As I parked my car at the funeral home the next day, Emily and her family pulled up alongside, and we walked in together. Nancy, Nancy, and Emily hugged and then moved off with their own families.

Tony came over. I thought perhaps he had softened, but he said to Emily, "Try to be inconspicuous." *Right*, I thought. By the time the service began, nearly a hundred mourners had gathered.

Tony acted more agitated than bereaved and, as the service progressed, his eyes shot daggers at me, trying to get me to hurry along. Jean deserved better than that.

Finally, I asked if anyone would like to share their memories of Jean. One after another, people stood and related stories about her, stories we had never known, good stories. I gave one more invitation when everything seemed to be winding down. Nancy the Elder, who had been adopted out at birth, walked to the microphone. She fit in perfectly with the mostly Scandinavian congregation.

She began speaking. "I would like to thank Jean for giving me life." Then she went on to make several positive comments about Jean. Her words went mostly unheard by people who were beginning to wonder what food would be served at the reception. She left the podium.

I looked up and was somehow not too surprised to see Emily marching down the aisle, all six-feet-three of her. She paused a second, and then said, "My name is Emily N'Gigi, and Jean is my birth mother." She stood even straighter and taller.

The room was filled with murmurs as people glanced at each other. Tony looked like a volcano that was about to erupt. Emily related the story of how a few years before she had located Jean and then, after telling everyone how courageous Jean had been to give birth to her, she confidently returned to her seat.

Before I could say another word, Nancy the Younger came to the microphone. She nervously swept back her curly Italian locks with her fingers. "I would like to thank my mother for giving me two wonderful sisters," she began and then proceeded to talk to her sisters about the joy they had brought her since they discovered each other. Tony continued to fume.

As we filed out of the sanctuary, I said to Tony, "That was a wonderful tribute to Jean."

"Well, some of it was," he snapped back.

We no sooner stopped in the foyer when a woman who had attended the service threw her arms around Tony.

"Oh, you wonderful man, the way you have accepted Jean's daughters is an inspiration to us all." Tony's face held an expression of total confusion.

Men shook his hand and said they admired what kind of person he was. Other women cried when they told him how much they loved him for having supported Jean when she was found by the daughters she had given up for adoption.

One woman even kissed his cheek as she hugged him close, and whispered in his ear, "God bless you, you saint of a man."

Within five minutes Tony was strutting around, his chest puffed out, glad-handing everyone he could reach, and reveling in his new-found celebrity.

The sound of a truck pulling up to the grave site brought me back to the present, and I looked at my nieces, Nancy, Nancy, and Emily, still holding hands.

"Sisters?" Emily said.

"Sisters," Nancy and Nancy answered.

Flo Golod *Fiction 2nd Place*

The Inventory

"Ask yourself, 'How am I feeling physically, mentally, emotionally and spiritually?'"

Lying in this familiar fetal position, the same safe curl my body finds before sleep, I try to consider the question as calmly as Jamie poses it at the end of Friday yoga class. In the last hour, my old body has been a swan, a warrior, a down dog, a tree and several other unlikely manifestations. I'm tired but oddly rested and my breathing is even and slow, just as the discipline suggests.

Having spent most of my life avoiding the topic of spirituality, I am pleased that Jamie starts the inventory with the physical.

I am physically fine, as long as I stay fetal. Once vertical, gravity and six decades will have their say with my joints. My knees will hurt, my leg may ache, and my neck will make noises like cracking knuckles when I move it from side to side. On the other hand, I can now do most of the poses that at first seemed so strange and hard. I was under the impression that yoga was relaxing and unpleasantly surprised when I found that my body didn't like any of it at first. When I complained, a friend given to irritating pronouncements reminded me that it's "use it or lose it time." Over the last year, I've learned that some of it does feel good and what hurts at least feels righteous. So, if I don't anticipate the aches and pains that will inevitably creep back, physically I'm swell.

On to mental. I consider the distinction between mental and emotional. This has confused me for a long time. Mental is thinking and emotional is feeling, right? But then there's mental illness or mental health. What I have learned from thousands of dollars and hours of therapy is that emotions recognized and named are healthy, albeit frequently uncomfortable and disorienting. Illness occurs when they are ignored or suppressed. Or you go crazy, which doesn't seem to have anything to do with good or bad emotional habits.

Since I can't resolve the dilemma and since emotion comes after mental in the inventory, I figure that I'll proceed with a narrow approach to mental, having to do with thought and memory. Am I mentally alert? An hour ago, I left my gym bag in the car, left the Y card in a different bag than the gym bag, and had to go back to the water fountain three times with a cup because I forgot my water bottle. I couldn't remember the name of the woman with the lotus blossom mat who introduced herself to me last week. But, lying here on my side with thirty other seekers, my head is clear.

Emotionally? Looking back on my life, I have been in a muddle much of the time. Psychological explanations abound. I've always favored them. So here's a shout out to all that therapy. Thanks to some skillful shrinks and all this stretching and breathing, my current list of anxieties (my credit cards, unhappy adult children, the aforementioned aches and pains, the rising sea level), and resentments (noisy neighbors, self-absorbed friends, the mediocre candidates for mayor), ebb and flow without so much drama. After an hour of yoga, there are no knots in my stomach and I'm not muttering under my breath.

Now is the moment of inventory reckoning. How am I spiritually? When I was young, I rejected church and avoided the spiritual movements of the time. Church was hierarchy, rules and the source of guilt. Guilt was a very bad thing since it was said to interfere with your sex life. Spirituality was induced by drugs or hawked by smug men emanating waves of Patchouli Oil, or white women who seemed to think they were Indians. I preferred the rationalists. Whatever their limits, they didn't try to sell anybody anything.

I figured I could live a long, useful and occasionally happy life without a spiritual basis until my friends started dying. I had not anticipated that a reasonable level of mental health would be insufficient in the face of grief.

So, lying on my side and breathing deeply, I consider Maggie. The cancer came back, this time in her lungs. Maggie, too, does yoga or did it. Now she's too tired. Maggie pursues a spiritual life, a pan-spiritual stir-fry of goddesses, rituals and this and that from more conventional religions. Hopes were high that with all that medical poison, plus the endless alternative therapies and her spirit path, she would get better. Now she's mostly exhausted, sick and scared, and I'm not sure if or how these spirits console or guide her. When I saw her last week she looked like hell and cried most of the day.

Nor is she being particularly accepting about this dying business. She's got books to write, lectures to give, gardens to plant and an eco-museum to build. She is the Goddess of Projects. So I wonder what kind of an arbitrary and inconsiderate deity says, "Close up Maggie's book now. She's done." My Catholic grandma used to say, "Well, his time had come." She was big on God's will.

I try testing my will against God, goddesses, even fate. I'll take on any contenders. I breathe with purpose and force. I breathe for Maggie, wanting to donate some of my not-yet-used-up life, bargaining for an exchange, more time for her and I'll knock off a few months or years of my allotment.

In my fetal clarity, I close my eyes and see that Maggie will die soon. I breathe and my aching heart clutches her, begging her to stay.

In those old movies, when someone boards a train and waves through the steam as the giant wheels begin to turn, the person left on the station waves, smiles and wipes away a tear. The train is taking the dear one so far away.

Jamie is suggesting that we roll slowly up from our fetal positions, cross our legs and, "Sit a little bit straighter with your mind a little bit clearer." I roll up and look sideways in the mirror. My corporeal self is sitting up straighter. Hanging onto Maggie as she fades, my other selves realize she'll soon turn up in my dreams. I breathe her in and, breathing out, say goodbye, for now.

"Namaste," says Jamie.

"Namaste," echo thirty other voices, some in whispers, some quite bold.

Gathering Glory

No longer on a road trip. No longer
necessary to zip on leather chaps,
suit up in armor jacket, pull on
gloves and a helmet with a shield
(just in case the sky decides to fall).
No black boots or wrap-around sunglasses.

No more monotonous buzz of motor
as tires skim between mesmerizing stripes
and solid lines. No aim for sweet spots.
No more chrome pipe rumbles
or cough of congested exhaust.
No cool air or summer heat fans cheeks.

No more tickle belly hills,
construction barrels dodged
or dirt roads navigated. No more
sudden exits or towns to blink and miss.
No more sawdust smell of new hewn lumber.
No Rorschach bug splats on windshield.

No more tanks sloshed with smelly gas
or red and blue lines snaking across maps.
No more must-see places visited
or lava fields too hidden to find.
No more grottos or auto shows toured,
no fry bread or Voyageur Rendezvous marveled.

No more firemen's pancake breakfasts,
no No Vacancy motels or overpriced hotels.
No more Blueberry Festivals or art shows.
No pictures to take or rest stops to make.
No coffee breaks or emergency roadside stops.
No getting lost or ah-ha finds around the bend.

Back to normal life, to driving behind glass
on four wheels, no longer part of the scenery
or one with the wind. Hawks won't drop
into ditches with prey in talons, eyes riveting you,
nor does road kill rot or skunk scent hover,
but glory clings like road grit under skin.

Heikki: 1860-1930

Midway to the farmstead
where our sheep are pastured,
we pause in the country schoolyard
for hurried moments on the monkey bars.
On this day of sweltering heat, thirsty sheep
wait at the moss-covered wooden water trough
where we will pump until they have their fill.
We make a game of our tiring task—
ninety-seven, ninety-eight, ninety-nine—
each in turn pumping one-hundred strokes,
counting aloud as the iron pump handle
becomes heavier and heavier.

No one lives here now—
darkened windows, silent house.
The sauna knows not the crack
of cold water on a bed of rocks
or the warmth of soul-satisfying steam.
We come only to tend the sheep
in this rugged pasture
where rocks protrude among hillocks
and lie scattered among the trees.
And we never stop to wonder about
the man whose home this used to be.
Just a name. Heikki.
Dad's immigrant uncle
who lies beneath the wind-blown pine
at the north edge of the country cemetery,
a weathered boulder as his headstone.

Richard Fenton Sederstrom *Poetry*

Family Chat

"She's worse," he says, like that,
but not worse than what.
We don't express our feelings much,
or well, around here.

"She's worse.
She's been kind of out of it, these last four days,
so we're taking her to the hospital."
We go back down the hill.

Nancy would have asked what we might want to drink.
"We have some lemonade, I think,
and maybe a Coke. Iced tea?
Jim, do we have iced tea?"

"You want a cup of coffee?" he'd ask instead.
"No, thanks." We'd sit on the couch,
answer the annual questions, mostly
about the brothers I've hardly seen in years.

Together we'd intone the memorial to last winter's weather,
"But maybe we'll have snow this year, finally."
We'd shrug in solemn agreement, nod, almost smile,
step out the door again.

Audrey Kletscher Helbling *Fiction Honorable Mention*

The Final Chapter

Clara swirled her hands in the dishwater, suds soothing fingers as the cotton dishrag circled the plate. Wash, then rinse. She worked in a steady rhythm, remnants of spaghetti sauce vanishing from fork, from kettle, staining the cloth orange.

In minutes she had completed the task, pulled the plug, rinsed the sink, draped the rag atop the faucet. The entire afternoon stretched before her now, unimpeded by responsibility.

Shuffling across the yellowed linoleum past the dining room windows toward the living room, she observed the wind whipping snow, muddling her view of ramblers set in tidy rows. Louisa, directly across the street, would be settled into her rocker, clasping cloth while she stitched a precise pattern of crossed threads. Next door, Clark would be slumped in the recliner napping, newspaper splayed upon his bulging belly. Van, on the corner, likely would be perched within feet of her television, mesmerized by some mindless game show.

None of this—not the crafting, the news nor the TV—interested Clara. As she eased her eighty-year-old bones into a glider rocker, Clara longed to escape the pinching pain in her spine and the bitter cold and ice of winter that locked her indoors.

Life hadn't always been this hard, in the sort of difficult way age and arthritis decreased her mobility and made her vulnerable. Once she'd nurtured three children. She'd cared for her husband, Ed, ten years her senior, until he suffered a stroke. He died in a nursing home two years ago, still bitter at her for placing him there. She'd served on the Lutheran Ladies Altar Guild and delivered Meals on Wheels and tutored first graders in reading.

But then, in the proverbial instant, Clara's life changed when she slipped on a patch of ice and spiraled to the ground. After hip surgery, she found herself in the very place Ed had despised. She declined Elsa's invitation to move in with her and Charlie in distant Cincinnati, knowing her youngest daughter possessed neither time nor patience. Her other daughter and son lived even farther from Minnesota and, like Elsa, had no interest in caring for their elderly mother except, perhaps, out of a sense of duty. So Clara pretended she would be just fine in a place where the underlying odor of urine stung her nostrils and old men called out in the middle of the night.

After six weeks institutionalized, as Clara referenced those recovery days, she returned home less sure of herself, although she was careful to hide her fears and bouts of confusion. She stopped volunteering, made up excuses to skip lunch dates with friends, ventured only to church and the nearby grocery store, post office and Edith's Used Bookstore, and seldom during the winter. She phoned often for meal delivery and stayed put, shut away in her house by a fear of falling.

Clara's days began to follow a predictable pattern dominated by hours tucked into her rocker reading books pulled from the volumes she'd purchased.

She'd never meant for this to happen—this opening of the clasp on her black leather purse, the parceling of bills and coins—each time she visited Edith's Used Bookstore prior to winter settling in. But, as she fingered worn spines and turned pages, the words drew her in. Oftentimes, after she carted an armful of books home, she'd bookmark pages and return to the bookstore full of questions.

"Have you heard anything about Carol?" Clara whispered to Edith one afternoon in early October. She didn't like to gossip, but she worried about Dr. Kennicott's wife.

Edith peered over her reading glasses, concern furrowing her brow. Clara took Edith's silence as a hint that she didn't wish to discuss Carol's tenuous situation.

Several weeks later, Clara inquired about Pastor Ingqvist and the visiting Lutheran pastors aboard a sinking pontoon. "How could that have happened?" she quizzed the shopkeeper. Edith just scowled at her in that dismissive way which caused Clara to simply turn and exit the store as the bookseller mumbled something about confusion.

Clara expected, though, when she approached Edith on a return visit in late November—the final one of the season, before winter kept her mostly indoors—that the bookseller couldn't possibly ignore her worried question about six bodies discovered in an underground mine on the Vermilion Drift. "Have the police arrested anyone yet?" Clara asked, boring directly into Edith's eyes.

But Edith stared at her in that unsettling way again, causing Clara to wonder if she really had any clue what happened outside her bookstore.

Kirstin Ruth Bratt *Poetry*

What we need now

What we need is a handbook for
grieving limbs for how to live on
without them for how a person
should look and see should listen or

look away when they come back when
they come among us work along
side us get to know us we're wrong
because we weren't brave we stayed on

home avoiding truth we need strong
neighborly rules governing poor
behavior they went we stayed then
they came home and there's a test for
two sides one oblivious one
without comfort still and how long

The Wall

Name after name of those who died
in a far-off jungle war are etched in granite,
a wall to justify death, the names
of those that politicians call fallen heroes.
But there is no wall, no memorial
for those who came home, eyes open,
bodies alive, souls dead,
got drunk and stayed that way thirty years,
strewing the wreckage of failed marriages
and neglected children in their wakes,
taking decades for these dead souls
to leave bodies ravaged by misery
married to guilt and shame.
On the wall I've built in my heart
I trace your name with my finger daily.

Charmaine Pappas Donovan *Poetry*

First Dance

for Helen Keith Beaman (1935-2011)
She died at home sitting in an easy chair
her sling a blue triangle Velcroed over one shoulder.
An uncomplicated operation she was told, routine.
Her daughter waited at the hospital to drive her home.

I see her pale makeup-free face dazed by anesthesia,
her frowzy hair matted from lying in surgery.
Nausea on the ride home kept her attention
to the car's interior as scenery whizzed by windows.

A startled look on her face is only momentary.
Now nodding, she offers a hand to the large stranger
as she would clutch the hand of any dance partner,
so they may twirl away beyond sass and circumstance.

Tim J. Brennan *Creative Nonfiction Honorable Mention*

What I Know about Alzheimer's

I am no longer acquainted
with you.
When you speak to me
I do not know
what to say.

What I know about Alzheimer's leads me to believe that Dad's passing, while traumatic, was a blessing. This acknowledgment remains difficult to admit, but it's true. Alzheimer's is a terrible affliction, and thinking "like father, like son" scares the living *bejeebers* out of me when I think about my own future.

My siblings had suspected for months Dad had Alzheimer's (e.g., a retired radio commercial salesman, Dad was caught more than once writing new radio ads for old accounts). Mother had passed in 1999 and, on this summer night, I had my Wisconsin dad in my Minnesota home for a visit. We put Dad in our finished basement, but he had come up the stairs at two a.m. one night because he couldn't remember where he was. He had one of my suitcases. Later, I opened it and found bathroom hand towels. It was my first experience of not knowing what to say to an Alzheimer's dad.

I wonder sometimes
if you remember
the birch trees
from the Beach Road house.

They walked at night, moving
to different locations
in our yard, trying to warn us
about the future.

The scene unfolded like some kind of black-and-white B-movie. I am convinced people who are afflicted with Alzheimer's even think in black-and-white.

"Dad, it's me, Tim." I touched his arm. "It's OK. You're at my house." His expression was wild, confused. It was the same look he had on his face the night before he died when he yelled at me to ". . . get the hell out of my room" because he was again in a strange place. I learned to recognize this look as one of preservation, instinct. That look reminded me of the conversation in Ron Howard's movie *A Beautiful Mind* when Dr. Rosen tells Alicia (in reference to her husband's psychotic behavior), "Imagine if you learned all the people, the places, the moments most important to you were not gone, but worse, had never been. What kind of hell would that be?" Dad's eyes looked like that kind of hell.

He did calm down that night, and I took him back downstairs and tucked him in like he must have tucked me in back in the day. Eventually, we had Dad committed to a Memory Home.

> *The one at the corner*
> *looked like a naked corpse,*
> *like you look now: white*
> *leafed hair, black spots*
> *on slender branches.*

Dad's present soon became only his past. It was as if nothing in the last twenty-five to forty years had happened. Oh, he knew me as a person he could trust, lean on, but the fact he never spoke my name the last two years led me to believe I didn't really exist for him. I was like small change he could carry around in his pocket. On my trips to visit, I would ask Dad what he wanted to do for the day. His always reply? "Let's get the hell out of here." And so we would. Off we would go for hours and miles. He loved to tour, to see the sky, the birch trees of northwestern Wisconsin.

One such trip in the early spring before he died, he turned to me and asked, "Is my mother still alive?" Again, I didn't know what to say to him as a son, so I explained in my best teaching voice that no, his mother had died many years ago. I was maybe four when his mother died and, although I didn't remember much about the funeral, I did remember that same sad expression on his face after I answered him. He never asked me that question again, and I actually chalked that up as a positive. Alzheimer's makes both sufferer and visitor think strange and ironic thoughts.

We played cribbage often at the Memory Home. It was one of our favorite games and he still liked to play. When we played, Dad would count both forward and backward. Our games would go on for hours and no one really won. I know with Alzheimer's that things like that didn't matter anymore.

I remember cutting it down
in 1972. It was diseased,
and you said it was the right thing
to do.

Before he slipped into the impossible, Dad told me a story back in 2007. He was exhibiting odd behavior even then, but nothing that led me to believe he was going to drift away from me forever. In this story, he told me of going AWOL in 1952 from basic training in Kansas in order to meet my mother in Iowa, she coming by train from Minneapolis to meet him halfway. He told me how he went to the wrong depot and how late he was arriving at the correct one to meet his new bride; how she was the only one in the depot, patiently waiting for the next train, and how he sat down behind her and just watched her for ten minutes, and how beautiful she was. He told me that same story at least thirty or forty more times after we all realized he was sick and yet, I never tired of how he told it . . . the details, how clear they were; how Mother's hair was set back in a bun, the blue-and-white dress she had on; the time of day, the sunlight across her back.

> *We cut it into smaller pieces,*
> *stacking them like body parts*
> *against our cellar door.*

Dad passed away from an aneurysm on May 5, 2009. From what I know about Alzheimer's, I was glad. As a son, I regret saying this and I regret thinking this but, also as a son, I believe it. Such is the paradox of Alzheimer's.

Marbles

She takes the old blue canning jar with the wire lid down from the long shelf. Her wrinkled, dimpled fingers carefully pull the wire lid off the mouth of the jar. The rubber seal pops like a cork report from a bottle of victory champagne. As she looks into the jar, a rush of memories: swirls, minnies, solids, and shooters. She sees the vacant lot and her friends from grade school. It's Saturday and the neighborhood kids are itching for a grand marble tourney. Two groups hold court on two of the marble playing fields: one, a flat patch of dry August grass, the other, an asphalt four-square play area with worn yellow lines. Through the course of the last few summers, the marble battles rule, halting only for rain or the call for supper. She realizes how everyone wins and breaking even is a standing tradition. As autumn and school eventually call, the kids compare the small, glass globes. For a few moments, their faces are caught in the swirl of spheres, multi-hues with suspended threads of color. She still sees the mystic fortunes in every little crystal ball, a little world swept up in every "cat's eye." Her face warms in the dim bulb over the basement shelf. She is lighter, shining brighter inside, a whorl of color as she carefully settles the jar in the row of the many others on the top shelf.

Margaret M. Marty *Poetry*

I Thought It Was You

I sat on the swing today—
you know—the one
on the screen house deck
where we always sat
as the full moon rose.

I thought I felt your arm
encircle my shoulders,
but it was the honeysuckle vine,
now grown
taller and thicker.

I thought I heard your voice
whispering in my ear,
but it was the wind
in the branches of that pine
we planted years ago.

I thought I inhaled your scent,
making me tipsy,
but it was the rich, dark earth
to which you have
returned.

Behind the Silver

They're back behind the silver,
transparent as stories
written on glass,

all the women
who used to show up
in my mirror.

Sometimes I see them—
the tired one
trying to distract a fussy baby,

the one with center-parted hair
so long it tangles
in her dangly gypsy earrings,

the pumpkin-faced child
grotesque from a flashlight
jammed beneath her chin.

They're still there
singing off key,
dancing the boogaloo.

Tomorrow,
or later this afternoon,
I will join them.

Another face, older,
will take my place
and laugh.

Jeanne Everhart *Poetry*

Shape of the Wind

My sister and I run barefoot;
our white legs beneath
flour sack floral print cotton
wait for a wisp of breeze
to billow sundress skirts.

The homemade quilt
in the oak tree shadow
is our refuge from the sun.
We stir small whispers with pleated paper fans
across strands of long hair sticking on damp faces.

I attach wishes for relief
to leaves hanging silent,
dandelion fluff balls wait patiently for
a breath of wind to carry seeds away,
drifting this hot Minnesota day into memory.

Too soon snowflakes swirl into drifts
defining the shape of the wind.
I remember youth's summer day
as I pull my warm wrap tight around old bones
and think how quickly yesterday blew past.

Susan Kathleen Spindler *Creative Nonfiction*

My Dining Room

No one else would call you church. I know that you are technically not. I painted your walls Louisburg Green five years ago. On one of them hangs an abstract I love. Vivid reds and the aquamarine of a moving ocean. I still don't know what it is exactly: Hares bounding? Dancers exiting stage left? Hard to tell. No matter.

The ceiling light, meant to hang dead-center, does not. Consequently your oval oak dining table will look misplaced no matter where it stands. The duet of balance and variance sings.

Your best asset is the large window overlooking the pond, the reason I bought the house. The first time I stood in you, I received a clear message. It was as if spoken in my heart: *you can heal here, Susan. Get a pen. Do a purchase agreement. You don't need to see the rest of the house.* So many hours, all these years later, I have spent writing in the graciousness of your warmth. At the oval oak table. I write for clarity. For clearance. For grief and forgiveness. Surely you are a hostess of healing.

Stories have come and I have filled journals. Poems rise from the underground, like the buttery daffodils I see turning their heads toward the sun ascending over the pond each new spring morning.

There are stories too that are not mine, but are here. Lucky, the huge wood-duck floats on the pond. His wife Lucy, killed by a fox in our neighbor's yard. It took most of the neighborhood in five canoes to round him up that first year and send him to the farm for his winter vacation. Perhaps his resistance to leaving was so adamant because he did not want to leave the place he had last seen his beloved Lucy. He fell in love again at that farm that winter. The two of them came back the next spring, transported in dog kennels in the back of my neighbor's Dodge Caravan. Within days they found a favorite spot on the south bank of the pond and cuddled there in the sunshine each morning, the two of them tender with each other, like new love is.

And the story of you. Your previous owner, drunk one night, did not brake when entering his garage. The car crashed through the wall that now holds the abstract. Small wonder the hares are jumping.

So, why do I call you church? The splash of sunlight through your window each day is not filtered by stained glass windows. The meals served here are to loved ones, not the sacraments of bread and wine.

But here you are, so large a part of my life. In you, I stop, I look. I see the choreography of autumn leaves floating like tiny parachutes; I see the ice glaze on the lake, and the hockey nets soon after. I see the infant green buds shining in a spring rain. You have made me see endings and beginnings in a new way. You have shown me life and its constancy and its steadfastness and its beauty and its pain. I am grateful. I am in awe. This is prayer. And surely, this is church.

Out of Line

Printed words are bound to lie
Flat, deadtrapped in dry ink on arid paper plains.
They heap up in lines, cracked, rigidblack,
Deserts to confound the furrower's blade and seed
So meaning blows off the top like dust, chaff, lies.

As when I was a willful child to be scolded, I am out of line.
Let me sing inkless and clear on a high blue sky,
Until the words fall, unbinding themselves
As the lines winnow down, free,
Reverting to simple fluid sound.

Scott Stewart *Poetry*

Once Was

emptied of immediacy

transient memories
darting
in out
up
down

hide and seek
seek and find,
lost and found,
quiet and loud
walk through the sky
float on the ground

shadowed persistence
lengthened
today
distanced tomorrow

Susan Niemela Vollmer *Fiction*

Waltzing

Joanne wasn't sure when she realized that Thomas was not her father. Maybe it was when she looked at the pictures of her parents' wedding reception in Aunt Lucille's photo album, and realized that the baby on Grandma's lap in the background was herself.

Maybe it was recognizing that while her brother Tommy had Thomas's short build and thin hair, she resembled neither parent, with her brown, curly hair and long-legged height. She might have heard something said, half under breath, about her not being Thomas's daughter.

For a long time, she said nothing. She had heard jokes about kids hoping that they were adopted because they didn't want to belong to their families. This was different. She wanted to belong, but she wasn't sure if she did.

Finally, one day in a fit of teenaged anger, she confronted her mother.

"Thomas isn't really my father, is he?"

Her mother met her eyes calmly.

"He isn't your biological father, but he is your father."

"Then who is my real father?"

"Your father was a ship that passed in the night. He was only here briefly and I've never seen him again. Thomas accepted that. This is our family." She spoke in the firm tone that she used in stating truths that could not be argued, like the lines in the Catechism that Joanne and Tommy memorized each week.

Then she turned a deaf ear to Joanne's pleas, sarcasm, and eventual tears.

Thomas was no more help. "Go ask your mother," he muttered.

"But I did, and she won't tell me. You need to tell me."

"I need to get the lawn mowed," replied Thomas, brushing past her.

Joanne began to watch them together. Were they really happy? Her mother tended the garden, cooked the meals, and visited with neighbors. Joanne wondered if these were the things she thought of, or was there a secret life playing like a movie in her head?

Thomas went to work at the mine, just as the other men did. He fell asleep in front of the television at night. Sometimes they played cards with friends. They kissed each other goodbye in the morning and hello each evening, and talked over cups of coffee.

Was this the life her mother had intended to live? What other life could she have had?

At her cousin's summer wedding, Joanne watched Caroline and Thomas move across the dance floor with grace and smoothness. Their rhythm was perfect, the steps in time, and they smiled into each other's eyes. They looked younger, more confident, like different people.

The next evening, she said accusingly, "I didn't know that you guys could dance!"

"Sure," Thomas answered. "Everyone from our generation danced every weekend. There were dances all over the place. Come here and I'll teach you." He held out his arms.

"One, two, three . . . No, you need to step back. Let me lead," he laughed. He guided Joanne patiently around the living room, counting, steering, ignoring her missteps.

"I'll never get it," she sighed.

"Keep practicing and it will come."

Thomas stepped into the kitchen and took Caroline into his arms, the dishtowel still in her hand. They glided across the linoleum, circling and dipping to music only they heard.

Still, Joanne could not give up her search. Aunt Lucille was vague. "That was a long time ago, hon. I really don't remember anything about him. Thomas is the only daddy you need."

"Nice girls shouldn't even think about such a thing," scolded Grandma. "Too much sex on TV. In my day, we knew enough to keep private things private."

Finally, Joanne stopped asking, but she never stopped wondering. She checked her birth certificate, but when Thomas adopted her, he was listed as her father. She listened to conversations at gatherings, keeping her ears tuned for some clue.

She wasn't sure what she would do if she did find out her father's name or where he lived.

"Hi, I'm Joanne. I'm your daughter. Caroline is my mother." He could be a millionaire, or a sleazy barfly. She wanted to know. She wondered if he had another family somewhere, if she had other siblings. How could he waltz into town, impregnate her mother, and then just waltz back out of her life?

When Joanne and Stan married and had children, her quest retreated to the back of her busy life. Then in one bleak year, Thomas died after a painful bout of cancer, followed unexpectedly by Tommy with a heart attack. Caroline fell on the concrete steps, and died without regaining consciousness. Aunt Lucille and Grandma were long gone. Joanne felt herself slipping to the bottom of the family tree—alone on a branch.

She began her questioning again, among older neighbors who might be able to give her a lead. Some didn't remember that Thomas wasn't her father. Several told her to leave well enough alone.

Finally, Mabel Warren gave Joanne her father's name. Mabel, who in the old pictures, wore high heels over silky stockings and suits with slender skirts and big shoulder pads, was shrunken and leathery now, tethered to an oxygen bottle. She and Joanne's mother had worked together before Joanne was born.

"Richard . . . Richard Peterson, that was his name. He was a salesman for a shoe company out of Chicago. We met him dancing. There were dance bands in Dee's Bar and at the Long Branch on the weekends. Caroline and I would get dolled up and dance all evening.

"Richard was one of those salesmen who passed through town twice a month on their routes. He was a good-looking guy—brown curly hair and he always wore a nice suit. All the men dressed well then. Suits and hats. Richard would buy us a drink, and he and Caroline would dance. Dance and laugh. We all laughed a lot then. We were so young.

"Anyway, he would walk us home afterward, or drive us in that nice black Ford. He'd always take me home first. I had no idea that anything more was going on. I only *danced* with the fellows." She scowled at Joanne and coughed a rattling cough.

Mabel wiped her mouth with a tissue. "When Richard came that last time, Caroline danced with him. After they dropped me off, she told him she was expecting. He told her he was married, and he took off like a scalded cat.

"She tried to find him. She even called the shoe company in Chicago. They said that he had left the company and they didn't have a forwarding address. I don't know if he had really left. He might have. Salesmen were pretty footloose in those days, but they might have been protecting him, too.

"Of course, she had to quit her job. It wasn't proper to have her working when she was expecting, especially since she wasn't married. So, she stayed at home and had you. No more dancing for Caroline. Her mother was so angry with her. That was the worst disgrace. For a girl to get pregnant was bad enough, but then not to be able to get the man to marry her was even worse. Your grandpa would have had his shotgun out if they could have found Richard.

"Caroline had known Thomas all her life. We went to school together. He started coming around after you were born, and pretty soon he wanted to marry her. They got married, and they had a good life. You need to let them rest in peace and quit asking questions."

Joanne hardly knew what she said to Mabel before she left. Her mind kept clinging to the names, Richard Peterson, shoes, Chicago.

With her children off at college, Joanne had long hours to search for her father. She scanned the Internet, paid for people searches, and haunted genealogy sites. She even drove to Chicago and searched for records.

And she found—nothing. There had been many shoe companies in Chicago at that time, and some were in business for only a few years. Few records remained. Richard Peterson was too common a name. There was a good chance that he was no longer alive.

Or maybe he was some old guy in a nursing home, who probably didn't even remember his own name, much less a girl named Caroline laughing on the dance floor.

Joanne knew that it was time to give up the search. She would have to be content with what she knew—a good-looking curly-haired married salesman laughed and danced with her mother one summer many years ago.

She thought of the tune of the Anniversary Song. As the lyrics and the sweep of the waltz filled her head, she saw not her mother and tall, handsome Richard Peterson, but Caroline and Thomas, work-worn, tender, waltzing in the dusky light of the summer kitchen.

Robert K. Anderson *Poetry*

Out of Loneliness

When, out of loneliness, the body moves
With brute assault against the soundless deep
That separates two souls, the moment proves
Too great for words. What's left to do but weep?
The silence tolls. Our frantic pawing stops,
As greedy lunge, hungry mouths, hearts that spin
Are stilled, and tender selves, defenses dropped,
Learn the limits of insinuating skin.
What's left to do but creep into his arms,
Take refuge in the rising, falling breath,
Steal from tentative embrace sufficient warmth
To stay the dark's admonishments of death.
Enough . . . this solace tells. What's left to do . . .
Is seize this generous solitude of two.

Marlys Guimaraes *Poetry*

Trying to Make Sense

His wife is alive, wedged between failing kidneys, a heart struggling to beat, fluid that builds in wrong places, mind clinging to clarity, feet that tremble in weakness. Some days the wheelchair replaces a walking wheeled frame. He left first, found on the bathroom floor, skin cold blue. A phone rings. "Can you come quick? He fell in the bathroom. I can't get him up," she speaks. She didn't know that a black-bagged gurney would take him from that room, followed by friends who lift and carry and lower his boxed body. We stood in the home for the dead, circling the box, on that day, a day of last looks. "He is not there, he is risen," the daughter says, seeing the body, emptied of spirit. An unbeliever does not speak, allowing them eternal visions as they grieve. Later, in quiet, he says, "He is not there; he is in you, your DNA."

David J. Thoelke *Poetry*

Icy Cold Water

Icy cold water, Superior don't drown me,
though my old boat is sinking and I can't see the shore.
Will any one wonder what's become of old Olaf
who left port in his old boat and was heard from no more?

I've taken your whitefish; I've taken your salmon,
taken your lake trout, any fish that you had.
I've fished from the springtime 'til deep in the autumn,
scraping a living, in good years and bad.

I loved being there in the harbor at twilight
with the sounds of Duluth and the birds in the air—
silhouette of the city against the soft sunset—
I wish just once more that I could be there.

I remember the times we would gather on First Street
'til late in the evening, then be up before dawn.
I've witnessed the sun rise across Gitchi Gumi
thousands of mornings, but now that's all gone.

I've felt the wrath of your winds in November.
I've fought through thick fog with some luck and some prayer.
The lighthouse at Split Rock has been my salvation,
but the beacon I loved so is no longer there.

Icy cold water, Superior you have me.
You're taking my body to become part of thine.
As I once told my darlin' as I stood o'er her gravestone:
"Dry land holds your bones, dear; let Superior hold mine."

Catherine Holm *Fiction*

Ferry Woman

Two days ago, under a gray autumn sky, Jackson quit his Minneapolis corporate job without notice. His heart had snapped shut. He'd felt the moment of it, the closing of a small spring-loaded box. *Is this what it's like?* he wondered. *Is this what it's like to have a realization?* Was it possible he had gone through his whole life without one realization?

His desk was spread with the remnants of a deal he was closing on with a bank in China. Up until that moment, it had given him a rush of pleasure to look at his soft leather high-back seat. His corner office had clean windows and a door. Up until that moment, the office had felt like a home. Cold wind had suddenly roared through Jackson, giving him the feeling of numbness and of flying all at once. He knew what he had to do. He took the only personal thing on the desk—a picture of his deceased Golden Retriever Pauly—and walked away.

Jackson's strides to his car felt like those of a giant. The sidewalks reverberated beneath his footfalls. He'd steered the Lexus north, planning to visit Minnesota's north shore, where he had vacationed years ago with his now ex-wife Trisha. But when he reached Duluth, a strange fit of spontaneity took hold. Jackson instead hurtled over the large bridge that crossed from Minnesota to Wisconsin, and into the town of Superior. He continued east on Highway 2, taking the turnoff to Bayfield. At Bayfield, Jackson squeezed into the last available room in a harborside motel. He fell into a deep sleep on the log bed, a red-squared quilt of loons covering his body.

Jackson stood on the Bayfield city dock, waiting for the sun to rise. Behind Jackson and up the hills beyond the town center, red maples blazed between old Victorian and brick houses. Jackson could not take his eyes off the calm water. Two elderly men stood at the end of the dock, leaning against the concrete wall with cameras perched on the railing.

"Morning," he said. They nodded and went back to staring through their cameras. Jackson wondered if they sat out here on the docks all day. Yesterday, he sat on a plastic Adirondack chair in front of his motel, watching the ferries shuttling people to and from nearby Madeline Island. Jackson had planned to go hiking on the island when he arrived at Bayfield. But he'd become so relaxed it never occurred to him to get on the ferry.

He had seen many couples here the past two days, strolling slowly through the shops, letting the energy of the lake wash over them. The town was a mix of well-to-do tourists, small shops, quiet, and the indefinable energy of the lake.

A woman stood on the dock to the left of him, leaning against the waist-high concrete wall, staring at the eastern horizon. To his right, one of the large ferries approached slowly from the island. It pushed through the water with a smooth and endless hum. Jackson marveled at its power. The thing was full of people, cars, even a logging truck full of logs.

Jackson was suddenly standing quite close to the woman. Had he moved? He didn't remember seeing her move. The ferry loomed large, pushing through the water, heading past the dock where he and the woman stood, to the ferry landing.

"It's hard to capture the sunrise," she said.

She was short like Trisha, but the similarities ended there. Trisha had fine facial features and hard eyes. This woman stared at him with fluid eyes that could drink him up. Her nose and lips were wide. She moved closer to him and he had the sense of the air around her dancing and moving with her.

"Come here often?" he asked.

She smiled. "You might say that," she said softly. The wind riffed her hair. Trisha's hair had never moved in the wind—it was too thick, wiry, styled. Trisha never stood in the wind.

"Let me take your picture," he offered, then immediately felt like a buffoon. What a predictable come-on line! But she leaned against the concrete wall, and the changing sky enveloped the world behind her. Purples, pinks, blues, white wisps of clouds. She closed her eyes and Jackson almost thought he saw her shift and flow, thought he saw her body move in a way that he'd never seen anyone move before. He snapped the photo as she smiled. He heard the hum of the ferry change to a deeper, smooth throb. Now, the plank would lower and the people would walk onto land.

"What's your name?" he asked.

"Tess," she said, moving to the side. He turned off the iPhone and put it in his pocket. Jackson turned to say something to Tess, and found her gone.

He walked away from the lake, turning toward the town. When he stepped over the place where the concrete dock melded smoothly with the pavement of the street, he felt a strange excitement. He walked two blocks up the hill into town and went into the grocery store on a corner on the right. There, he bought things he could prepare in his room, which included a small refrigerator, a sink, a microwave, and a few dishes and glasses and silverware. He had the feeling that he had seen enough of the town. All he wanted to do was be in his motel room, sink into the cushiness of a black futon, keep the TV off, the lights low, and listen to the sounds of the ferry coming in. He could look out the window through half-open shades and see the ferries as they pulled in and as they left. Every time the ferry lowered and lifted the plank that let people get off or board, the ferry made that deeper rumbling noise. Every time he heard that deeper rumble, Jackson's heart thrilled. He sat for hours on the futon, a half-eaten bologna sandwich on white bread forgotten on a plate.

At night, Jackson got up from the futon and left the half-eaten sandwich, opening the door. There was a fall chill in the air and the stars were thick in a clear sky. How had it become possible to go through life without the thrill in his heart he had felt here today? He sat in the Adirondack chair on the small lot of the motel. *I could stay here forever,* he realized. *I could stay here forever and never leave, live out my life watching the water, the sky, fed by the deep heartbeat of the ferry.*

He fell asleep in the chair, the cold air chilling his cheeks and nose, his legs tucked beneath him, his arms crossed tight around his chest to stay warm. Somehow he had forgotten about the motel building behind him, about his warm room and the sturdy log bed with a stylish quilt and the small refrigerator stocked with food. Somehow that had all dropped off the earth, and Jackson believed he sat upon an island of grass. Perhaps all the world consisted only of him and the chair and the huge lake that stretched out in front of him, the sky, and the ferry. He sat up straighter, looking into the direction of Madeline Island. The ferry was coming! He could hear its low and smooth rumble as it powered through glassy calm water. The darkness of the early morning was beginning to break up, and the pre-light of the coming sunrise beginning to break through the gray dusk. A pink line of light rimmed the long and vast horizon.

Jackson blinked. The ferry was suddenly very close; it seemed that it had skipped over the water. The hum drew him—he stood up, crossed the street, walked down a little grassy hill, walked across the landing parking lot, stood at the landing. No one joined him. The parking lot was empty of cars. A flag pole rope clanged in a sudden burst of wind, lashing against the pole. The ferry shimmered, and seemed to twist and sway like a mirage. Jackson had a sudden memory of his gleaming Lexus, propelling itself over the bridge to Wisconsin.

The ferry slowed, using reverse brakes and churning water backwards. And then the deep rumble came, the chord that played to Jackson's heart. The plank lowered—huge, dark, wide. The boundaries of the ferry shimmered, part of the water, part not. Nothing was hopeless, Jackson realized. He stepped from shore onto ferry, and a charge went through his body. Like running, seeing the world from above, understanding. The plank lifted behind him and the ferry backed out and steered out toward the big water, where Jackson would always be free.

Lina Belar *Poetry*

Boundary Waters Lament

The land near Ely was once tall-timbered
until they shaved the trees and
from the virgin soil a leaner look emerged,
like a woman whose naked skull
reveals stark beauty.

Instead of towering pines there is
this peach fuzz of new growth timber,
while tucked in the woods a solitary maple
spills color like blood
from a fresh wound.

George H. Johnston IV *Creative Nonfiction*

ER is a Lot Better on TV

I am writing this to counter the claims of those who say that I spent Tuesday and Wednesday in the psych ward. That's totally untrue. It was Wednesday and Thursday. No, no. That's still not true. The mostly true story is below.

Monday, I had a dull pain in my chest off and on all day. When I got home and got out of the van, it suddenly got much worse. I mentioned it to my wife and she decided that she didn't want to collect on my insurance, at least not my life insurance. Health insurance was another matter.

We decided to go to the hospital in the next county rather than the one in our county. My wife spent some time in the local hospital once. Once. Neither of us will go back for any reason including our autopsies.

Yes, I have completed my intensive, personal research into advances in medical technology for cardiac patients at a nearby hospital. My conclusion is that the advances are great, the care is thorough, and the process is frequently painful. Twice I had two EKGs going simultaneously. (I think it was twice; my memory is a little fogged due to lack of sleep.) One of the occasions I remember vividly because it required sandpapering off my skin. I had strong religious objections to the procedure. If God didn't want us to have skin, He wouldn't have given it to us. Those who maintain that my objection is because I am terrified of needles, knives, and pain are way off the mark.

I discovered that Monday night is a really bad night to go to the emergency room. The place was overflowing. I can see Friday and Saturday nights. I can even see Sunday night as people suddenly realize they need to return to work the next morning. But Monday night? Does a major portion of the population have an allergic reaction to work?

I also discovered that it is impossible to sleep on a stretcher in an emergency room. The staff kept telling me that they were looking for a room for me. I kept wondering whether they'd lost any rooms. I know the government has lost people and buildings but could a hospital lose a room? ("Paging Dr. Kildare. Paging Dr. Kildare. Please return Room 415. We need it.") Were they planning on discharging someone at 3 a.m.? Did they expect someone to pass away? Were they negotiating an accelerated construction contract to expand the hospital's capacity?

I was hooked up to more machines than exist in a typical city. At least one of my 5,317 leads was receiving messages from our Saturn probe. In fact, at one time I think I was receiving messages from Saturn. (It was something about how they were supposed to be the ones doing the probing, not the ones being probed.)

One monitor kept beeping every time my pulse fell below 60. Another beeped every time something fell below 10. (At that time of night, I think it was my IQ.) A third monitor tracked my blood pressure. I watched it drop to 101 over 47; then it, too, beeped, and showed a pressure of 0. Fortunately, it wasn't my blood pressure that had dropped off; it was my blood pressure cuff. I adjusted it and the monitor admitted that I was still alive.

The TV was on the whole time I was in the ER exam room since my control could only change the volume and the channels. At 3 a.m., the monitors were more interesting than the TV.

I was given a nitroglycerine pill and, later, a nitroglycerine patch. Who was the first to think: "Nitroglycerine is a very dangerous explosive. I bet it will make a great heart medicine." Did someone notice that people who handled large quantities of nitroglycerine almost never died of heart attacks? Did someone fail to notice that people who handled large quantities of nitroglycerine almost never lived long enough to die of heart attacks?

At 4:15 in the morning, someone found a room and I was moved to it. The nurses unplugged all my leads and plugged them into a portable monitor. The staff called it a wireless monitor but there were still plenty of wires hooked to me.

Doctors, nurses, technicians, and random visitors kept taking my blood, apparently under the theory that the less blood I had, the easier my heart's job would be. They also kept taking my medical history. I know cops like to keep questioning witnesses to see if their stories change but I had no reason to lie, except to lie down and that wasn't doing me much good, what with all the people taking my blood and medical history.

In the room, I fell asleep around 6:45 and wasn't awakened until 7 a.m. I then started a round of exams that lasted approximately as long as the average presidential campaign. It's a toss-up as to which is more irritating. I stood against walls and machines and lay in tubes. I was injected with more radioactive material than Spiderman, but I didn't get any of the cool superpowers, let alone the cool movie contract. I beeped my way through the halls and examining rooms.

At least three times, medical personnel started to interview me or report on results but not one of them completed two sentences before being paged. "The fifteenth electrocardiogram showed . . . " Buzz, ring, beep.

Late Tuesday afternoon, the doctors decided that they needed the room for someone else, possibly because Dr. Kildare still hadn't returned Room 415. The hospital discharged me and told me to go home and stop cluttering their halls.

By the way, after a couple of days in the hospital, my heart is now the most examined object in the known universe. It seems to be working. I did receive medical advice to reduce stress. And how am I supposed to do that while Congress still exists?

Renee Loehr *Poetry*

Repetitive

Coal black cattle,
Amid golden stubble
Like hairbrush bristles,
From a distance
Giant beetles.
Huge mounds of hay
Rolled up like pastries.
Tractors crawling
Through the fields
Plowing up what remains.
Miles pass on I-94
Through South Dakota
And the scenery
Repeats itself again
And again.

Mary Scully Whitaker *Creative Nonfiction*

TMI

I never know if I'll get a chatty or a private next to me on the plane.

Clearly, she purchased her ticket late or is not a frequent flyer, to be traveling alone, and relegated to the middle seat. I text myself signaling privacy, until the plane door closes, then grab Sky Mall during take off until I can open my computer.

She reaches over my arm and points to a product on the page, "I bought that, and it was a nightmare."

I grunt.

"It took three weeks for Hammacher Schlemmer to deliver it and then it didn't work and I had to send it back and it was another three weeks before I got the replacement."

I grunt. Already, too much information.

"I thought my boyfriend would love it, 'cause he's always asking me to give him a back rub."

I look out the window. Way too much information.

"But really, I think he just wanted me to touch him. I don't think he thought the massager was that good. It was expensive and it made his skin itch, he said."

I turn the page. Way, way too much information.

"I didn't think about how when I give him a back rub it always leads to sex. Kinda dumb, don't ya think?"

Yup, I think, but don't say.

"So, if you think you really want one of those, I'd sell you ours at a really good price, 'cause, like I say, we never use it."

"No thanks," I say.

"I wouldn't charge you shipping to send it to you. And really, it's very clean. Like I say, he only used it a couple of times."

I continue flipping through the pages of the catalogue.

"So now I know if he wants to have sex, especially during the day, maybe while we're watching football or something, he just says, 'Why don't you give me a back rub?' It's kind of his signal."

Oh god, this is way too much information.

WE HAVE REACHED CRUISING ALTITUDE. YOU MAY NOW TAKE OUT YOUR APPROVED ELECTRONIC DEVICES, AL-THOUGH CELL PHONE USE IS PROHIBITED UNTIL WE LAND.

I'm afraid to take out my computer. She'll look over my shoulder and climb into my business.

"My boyfriend and I are thinking of moving in together, but it's really a big decision, 'cause sometimes he's late on his rent or stays out all night with the guys drinking, and I don't think I'd like that."

Information I could have lived my life not knowing. I'm actually feeling sorry for the boyfriend. "I think I'll doze for a bit," I say and roll toward the window, close my eyes, not caring how uncomfortable I am.

She turns towards the aisle passenger. "Are you from here, or going home?" she says.

The Wolves, the Swans and the Fire-Breathing Dragons

Karen doesn't miss much. She possesses the child's innate affinity for wonder, and the eye of an artist. So I am a little surprised Karen does not see the orchids first. Perhaps she was scanning the shoreline or watching the family of trumpeter swans out on the water.

We are paddling on a lake deep in the Chippewa National Forest. A mile off the beaten path, we bounced from rut to rut before stopping in a grassy opening guarded by an ancient white pine. This lake and I are old friends. Years of acquaintance have cemented the bond between us. In the beginning I came here for the duck hunting. Now my need to have the feeling of being truly in the wild is why I return to this tree-lined shore.

Years ago while waiting for daylight to bring life to the world, a lone voice, deep and strong and sure, rose out of the black forest behind me. Swelling to a crescendo, the singer paused and began again. The memory of that wolf howling on a cold October morning remains long after the echoes faded into the dark silence. Sometimes curious otters bobbed up and down in the decoys, snorting with derision before swimming away. One morning the air was filled with the buzzing of powerful pinions as a pair of trumpeter swans passed over so low I could almost feel the beating of their wings. Their impossibly long necks and huge white bodies glowed against the background of dark gray clouds. I received these things as the gifts they were.

Few people visit this lake. The presence of man does not intrude here. I long for big empty places and the time to lose myself completely in them, but that is not always practical. For this reason I keep spots like this in my heart and close at hand.

We float in a world of colors and scents, of faultless blue sky and verdant sweetness. Our red canoe slips in and out of shadows cast by black spruce and tamarack. Sunlight is alchemized into gold and the resinous aroma of the wild; fresh and green and cool washes over us. Blue Flag Irises stand tall above the pink and white flowers of Bog Rosemary and Labrador Tea. The delicate beauty of their blossoms is rivaled only by their fragrance. Out on the lake the swans suspend without effort on a mirror reflecting two very different worlds. Surrounded by all these exquisite delights, it is no wonder Karen overlooked the fiery magenta of the orchids hidden in the mossy hummocks.

Like a pebble dropped into a still pond, our reverie is disturbed by a voice. "Wait a minute." Reaching with my paddle, I begin pulling our canoe back toward the orchids. The tea-colored water gurgles as we change direction. I do not tell Karen what I saw and she does not ask. I know Karen has spotted them when she gasps, "I think they're Dragon's Mouth."

I push our bow into the dense bog mat until we bump to a stop. Nearly hidden in the grassy sedges, several Dragon's Mouth orchids balance on thin stems. Karen giggles as she leans far out over the gunwale for a closer look. Sometimes these small things that enter our lives possess so much alluring beauty, it is difficult to resist the temptation to touch them. We are left to find other means to capture their intense presence. Karen reaches for the camera. When she has the photographs she needs, we swap places.

I've never actually seen a Dragon in the wild before. Just beyond arm's reach, pointy pink ears and flaming tongues of magenta and yellow mimic the fairy-tale beasts of childhood. Knowing what they look like, it is hard to believe we nearly missed their brilliant bursts of color in this sea of green. Backing the canoe out, we continue down the shore, watching everywhere now for small fire-breathing flowers.

Finding these orchids is just the beginning. While the nervous adults wait nearby, we investigate a loon nest. A pair of large speckled eggs lies cratered in a low mound of vegetation dredged from the shallow water. Karen's attention is focused elsewhere when the eyes of the first wolf meet mine. The brown face rises above sedges before turning away. A few moments later a black wolf stands broadside, then leaps into the anonymous safety of the swamp. Karen does not, however, miss the swan feather spinning across the water to her hand.

Rhoda Jackson *Poetry*

Insomnia

If only I could
Suspend the
Loquaciousness
Erupting from this
Earthly
Plateau
and
Dance in the
Realm of an
Ethereal,
Abundant
Meridian.

Miriam Kagol *Poetry*

Deep Dark Secret

She doesn't trust the power
of her inner voice, carves her lines
on the frozen surface, skates

across a winter pond always
and only with friends, swerves
away from the soft spot in the center

where the rotten ice might give,
cherishes the shoreline, keeps
coming back to touch the bank.

She dreams in uneasy sleep
of a time when she might be pulled
on hissing blades toward the open water

and sink into that dark, vivid
depth beneath, where a whole world
lives in secret.

Marlene Mattila Stoehr *Creative Nonfiction*

The Train to Hearst

Rumbling thunder dispatches us on our journey. We are 296 miles from Hearst, Ontario, and the cocoonish sanctuary of our railroad car gives promise of ten hours when weather, good or bad, can but enhance the mood of adventure.

When a family boarded carrying an odorous poodle with a screaming electronic toy, we shuddered. "He doesn't play with it much," the mother volunteered in response to my startled look. The father smoked a cigar before departure, and I feared that aroma, too, might linger. The second passenger car, we speculated, could not be worse. We share this space with two sleeping sweatshirt-clad passengers only.

Incorporated in 1899, intended to reach Hudson Bay but out of money at Hearst, the Algoma Central Railway serves canoeists, fishers, cottagers and tourists seeking a wilderness experience. Scarcely five miles from Sault Ste. Marie we plunge into a lush boreal environment. Branches brush windows and bushes obscure the forest floor. Here, where retreating glaciers scraped bedrock, trees soar to astonishing height with little in which to anchor their roots.

We inch through the spellbinding landscape, hearing the squeak of the platform between cars, the answering groan of the swaying floor beneath us, the clatter of wheels on rails. A mournful four-syllable train whistle announces infrequent road crossings. The forest itself is silent.

At one moment we skirt a wall of rock, at another we look up, down or out upon a dense woodland. Mile-marker posts allow us to chart progress on our timetable. At Mile 14 we pass through Heyden, the first of several flag stops on the route. No one from Heyden boards the train today.

At Mile 19 we cross an 810-foot-long, 100-foot-high trestle bridge. Our train, an engine, baggage car and two passenger cars, seems a miniature model and we miniature people, so high are we above the terrain. A higher and longer trestle lies ahead, the 130-foot-high, 1,550-foot-long span over the Montreal River at Mile 92.

At Mile 102 the train begins a descent into Agawa Canyon, terraced with multihued sediment deposited by melting glacial ice. We exit through a 50-foot-wide gap in solid rock. The railroad hugs the overhanging west wall while the river carves its way below the sheer east wall. This is the destination for one-day excursions, but we have the luxury of time, Monday to Friday, and anticipate additional wonders ahead.

Here forests close in, green rickrack wrapping first to one side of the track, then the other. Delicate tamarack, dark-needled spruce, fluttery poplars, tufted pine, and birch unfurling shaggy bark reach toward our window. The sky is blue with building cumulus clouds. Saucer-shaped lakes dot the landscape; room-sized rocks rise from muskeg swamps.

Maroon milkweed sparkles with morning dew, ruby-red raspberries ripen near clusters of pin-cherries, yellow black-eyed Susan bloom beside purple phlox. A fern forest grows beside the track, and a bark-bare log floats beside water lilies, green pads forming circles upon the still and stagnant water. A loon dives below a lake surface, its reverie disturbed by the passing train. A startled moose runs along the track, then escapes to the bush.

Passengers are picked up and dropped off, many at open-sided shelters. Two groups haul gear to a pontoon boat, where a canvas top gives only slight protection from a pouring rain. A disparate lot gets off at Mile 165, Hawk Junction, the most popular area for wilderness adventures.

At Miles 210 and 212 we cross the bridges of Squaw Bay and Hoodoo Bay, built on pilings driven into the muskeg. Skeletal trees, now only bare poles, generate jagged reflections in the water. A dead poplar stands upright, saplings encircling it as though performing a maypole dance.

At 7 p.m. we reach our destination, Mile 296, and walk across the train yard to the back door of the Companion Hotel. Hearst is a French-speaking town. The clerk greets us, then, recognizing our tourist status, switches to English. She apologizes. "I am sorry, my restaurant is closed for the civic holiday, but there is a Chinese place. I will check if it is open." We listen in amusement as she calls the Chinese restaurant and converses in French.

This is Hearst, where there is little to do and we do that for three days. We walk the length of this shoestring town on the Trans-Canada Highway, two miles long and four blocks deep, from the Welcome Center on the west to Maki Hardware on the east. In the paint store a man we learn is a teacher relates the town's heritage before the Finns left and the French came. He sends us to the hardware store to meet the only Finnish family left in town and the store's near-eighty-year-old owner. We read at the library; our hotel clerk says no one in town goes to the library to read. "We check out books and take them home with us." There is time for naps and aimless walks and a return to the Chinese restaurant. But soon it is 8:30 Friday morning and time for our return.

The conductor puts our suitcases "in this corner of the baggage car" because "lots of people will get on at Hawk Junction." We innocently settle into our private car. Station names click off in reverse order: Wyborn, Stavert, Coppel, Mead, Horsey.

Most of those "lots of people" who board at Hawk Junction are men sporting vacation beards, as odorous as the pet poodle that, to our displeasure, is again aboard. Four adventurers with a guitar begin to sing in loud twangy voices. I overhear snippets of conversation from four men, one dominating with poorly related tales. His mates teeter at the brink of sleep, feigned, I believe. Studying a hand-held GPS he suddenly declares, "There's a road coming up. There it is!" "This is a R-A-I-L-road," I scream, silently, then surrender to the situation as our train wends its way to Sault Ste. Marie's waiting depot.

Kathryn Knudson *Poetry*

Catching a Memory of Spring

The statue's feet anchor
in a drift,
            her face turned
    to the west,
                her bent knee
        exposing a thigh from the folds
            of a concrete toga.

Catching a memory
            of spring, her delicate arms
    lift a basket
                mounded with snow
    as if today's
weak sunlight might be
                strong enough to
        melt her burden.

LuAnne White *Poetry*

The Gardener

In her labyrinthine garden
from earth, from sky
from water, from sun—
a small seed
warms.

A tendril up, a rootlet down—
two small spirals
twisting towards light and dark—
push to freedom, press to nourishment—
growing bolder both
from dark of moon
to fullness in time.
Lovely magenta blooms
going to seed under a Blue Moon.

She stands nearby
drawing in moonlight with every breath—
gathering seed puffs,
feather light,
magenta kernels clinging to white fluff
perched on stems dying, set to fly.

Breathing out gently.
Blowing upwards and outwards.
Her breath lifts tiny beings
planting hope and joy wherever moon shines her light.

Humming a grateful tune, she smiles,
plucking the next seed pod
to release under the Blue Moon.

Halloween Moon

As I peered out the door, edginess flooded my body. It was midnight and I had drawn the short straw to let the dog out. The girls and I had just watched *Halloween III* in complete darkness.

Teddy was grousing, his tail beating against my leg. He meant now! Wishing he wore doggie Depends, I opened the door. He barreled past me, clearly on a mission. In hot pursuit, I stumbled down the stairs and into the chilly night.

Patches of fog obscured my view. A sense of foreboding coursed through my veins. Leaves rustled across the grass while wind gusts spiraled crispy strays. My slippers crunched those in my path. The maple tree by the driveway was shedding its leaves like powdered sugar through a sifter. Damp, musty air engulfed my nostrils, reinforced it was Fall.

Teddy was creating a flurry of activity. Leaving his mark on every tree, he darted in and out of the fog. Oblivious to my restlessness, he flew by chasing an airborne leaf.

"Come on, Teddy," I grumbled. "Do your business!"

He gave me his "You can't catch me" look and scampered down the hill. Trying to navigate the incline, I skidded like an unsteady skier on a bunny slope. Teddy was waiting at the bottom, furry snout lifted mid-air, projecting a sense of grandeur. Delusions of grandeur was more like it.

"Who? Whooo."

A sound pierced the air as though it were a special effect in an eerie horror movie. Teddy was suddenly attached to my pants like Velcro. I patted his side reassuringly. I glanced across our pool fence; there stood "Old Faithful," the gnarled oak tree that had survived many a Minnesota snowstorm and had scorched bark from numerous lightning strikes.

Branches had seared off portions of the rotting trunk. Year after year, Mother Nature surprised us. Buds appeared and burst into avocado-green leaves.

The mist slid across the prairie. A Halloween moon hovered behind the old tree.

Its illumination seemed almost ghoulish. Pumpkin orange, it shone on the arthritic-looking limbs. Nestled on a creaky branch sat an intimidating barn owl. His enormous, haunting eyes pierced the darkness.

"Who? Whooo," he hooted again.

Teddy began barking. His head peeked out between my knees. This tough guy persona was a ruse. His quivering confirmed otherwise. Unexpectedly, there was a whooshing sound overhead. The lone owl took flight. The majestic presence emerged in the moonlight.

"There . . . you scared him away, big guy. Now can we please go inside?"

I didn't have to ask twice. He tore up the hill as though an invisible cattle iron had prodded him. I trudged after him. My warm bed beckoned me.

Blood-curdling howls shattered the silence. Coyotes. The infamous creatures were known for stalking their prey at night. They answered each other in a creepy off-key chorus. Teddy recoiled in fear. I attempted to reassure him. They weren't a threat. He knew I was lying. Neighbors had reported being confronted while walking their dogs during the day. Imagine the threat they'd pose in the dark.

Like a flash, they darted past the trunk of Old Faithful. Their mangy figures were a mere thirty yards away, the shaggy coats illuminated by the orange hue of the moon. They were practically a stone's throw away. Obviously Teddy's barking had summoned them. I was unarmed, not prepared to do battle. Where was my husband's handy crowbar when I needed it?

I grabbed Teddy's collar and we bolted toward the house. Scenes from the horror movies *Cabin in the Woods* and *Wrong Turn* flashed through my mind as we skirted inside. As I slammed the door, my heart pulsed. Maybe Walkers from *The Walking Dead* were hunting us too. My breathing was labored. No more scary movies this Halloween season. Maybe it was just a sugar high from the trick-or-treat candy we had been inhaling. My pulse returned to normal. Teddy licked my hand reassuringly.

Wait . . . I was letting a pack of coyotes intimidate me? I don't think so! We'll see who is tougher. Throwing open the garage door, I went in search of the perfect weapon.

An aluminum bat is now propped by the back door. Who would have thought discarded pumpkins would make such great target practice? Among the local coyote cartel, I am known as the "Sultan of Swat."

Marlene Mattila Stoehr *Poetry*

They Also Serve

(After John Milton's *On His Blindness*)

Her scarecrow,

her loyal companion,

waits in her garden each day.

Not a dashing fellow,

expression unchanging.

A ragged shirt

hangs loosely on his jack pine frame,

flapping freely in any breeze,

fading in the summer sun.

Shoes? He has none.

Hat? Once yellow straw,

now brittle-brown and tattered.

On the job. Stalwart. Stationary.

Never hoeing weeds or digging potatoes.

Neither adding to the rock pile

nor harvesting bounty.

But loyal he is. Patient. Silent.

Serving as he was meant to serve,

waiting in her garden each day.

Poster Duty Diary

Friday, 9:10 a.m. I'm all prepared and excited to get started on my first Publicity Committee assignment: hanging posters for the Annual Public Parks Party Fund Raiser. My new lime green garden tote is filled with matching lime green thumbtacks, forty colorful 9x12 posters, a staple gun, extra staples, Scotch and masking tape.

Friday, 2:30 p.m. Finished! I politely asked permission to hang my posters at every site and approached each location like an art project. I neatly rearranged all the other ads, notices and posters to create an advantageous spot for mine. It was a bit embarrassing at the drugstore when I moved the ad for:

PERK UP, A NEW REMEDY FOR A COMMON MEN'S PERFORMANCE PROBLEM

I quickly tacked that ad to the upper left corner of the bulletin board where children would be less likely to read it.

Monday, 2:30 p.m. I was very irritated when I noticed that several other posters on the Community Bulletin Board were overlapping my Annual Public Parks Party Fund Raiser poster. It took me 30 minutes to rearrange everything but I must admit it looked much better when I was finished.

Wednesday, 4 p.m. I stopped at the grocery store this afternoon and couldn't believe my eyes. My poster was dangling by one lime green thumbtack and the other three lime green thumbtacks were now holding a scrawled sheet of crumpled, dirty paper stating:

DESPERATE HANDY MAN NEEDS WORK ANY JOB! (WEEKDAYS ONLY 10-4)

I tore DESPERATE down; then in a spirit of compassion, I used one of my lime green thumbtacks to attach "HANDY MAN" to the lower frame of the board. I neatly rehung my Annual Public Parks Party Fund Raiser poster.

Thursday, 10:30 a.m. Checked the Community Bulletin Board . . . HAD TO REARRANGE IT AGAIN! Then I drove to the printers for 6 additional posters to replace those that had completely disappeared from other locations. My blood pressure is still elevated over these breaches of poster etiquette.

Saturday, 12:30 p.m. I was buying more tape and lime green thumbtacks at the hardware store when I saw my Annual Public Parks Party Fund Raiser poster half covered by a notice with a large picture announcing:

Adorable, Fluffy, Lovable, Almost Litter-Trained Kittens

At the bottom was a row of about 15 tear-off phone number tabs. When no one was watching, I tore off every single one, threw them in the trash, repositioned my poster, came home and went to bed with a migraine headache.

Monday, 10 a.m. At the bank this morning, my Annual Public Parks Party Fund Raiser poster was almost completely covered by an ad for:

Sam's Super Sipper Sanitary Systems Service

As I moved it, I totally inked out Sam's telephone number with my permanent black marker!

Monday, 1 a.m. I've had trouble sleeping the last few nights and I've bitten off all my nails.

Tuesday, 2 p.m. While shopping at The Garden Center, I found my Annual Public Parks Party Fund Raiser poster torn down and discarded on the fertilizer bags. In its place was an ad announcing:

Maggie's done it again . . .
Presented us with 11 darling lab (mix) puppies.
These beautiful babies are looking for good homes.

$15 each, but free if you take 2

I yelled out loud, "Why don't they spay the poor dog?" as I grabbed their notice down, tore it into little pieces and threw it behind the fertilizer bags. I put a new Annual Public Parks Party Fund Raiser poster back where I had originally hung it.

Wednesday, 6 p.m. I replaced, resurrected or rearranged 11 posters today. I think I'm getting an ulcer.

Thursday, 1 a.m. My husband said I woke him up screaming, "Keep your blankedy-blankedy-blank cotton-pickin' hands off my posters!"

Thursday, 10 a.m. to 4 p.m. I drove around town, tearing down any ads, notices or posters even close to mine.

Thursday night. I tossed and turned all night!

Friday, 10 a.m. to 4 p.m. See Thursday.

Friday night. See Thursday night.

Saturday 10 a.m. to 4 p.m. The Annual Public Parks Party Fund Raiser was an <u>unbelievable</u> success. People actually saw my posters!

So next year I'm going to sign up for the . . . Food Committee.

Barbara Draper *Poetry*

Running with Smelt

Dark at night, my friends and I would tumble from cars—
smokes and beer, waders and nets—into the fast lane
of the river, into a fusion of headlamps and smelt,
into pandemonium flapping in nets. Sixteen.

Our scales were gaining color. Smelt raced
upstream while we prepped for the downstream race—
to the big lake. The big life. The city. Commonplace stars
blazed the sky and jitterbugged off the river,

while we worked our cool on cigarettes and stolen beer,
thinking not a wit about today, three decades later,
when a reunion beckons us back to the shore of Lake Huron
where the river tumbles in. To the river of stars

that didn't go out to sea. We circle the bonfire,
amazed how happy we are to shiver off our separateness
and swim close for the warmth of old friends
who remember the smelt that no longer run.

Mike Lein *Creative Nonfiction Honorable Mention*

Labrador Spring

I bring matches, firewood, a bucket of water, and a couple of craft-brewed beers to the first campfire of spring. Kaliber, the current Labrador Retriever-in-Residence, brings her favorite stick of the weekend, and her seemingly limitless energy. After a 4 a.m. wake up call and a long day of turkey hunting, I'm content to relax lakeside in a chair, feed the fire, and watch the spring wildlife show. She's ready to play.

My spouse Marcie and I have raised four Labrador Retrievers over the years, all of them black, and all of them female. The first three, Maggie, Brooke, and Ripley, had their personal quirks and their initial puppy energy. But they mellowed after two or three years and were content to be companions when hunting season wasn't in season. They asked no more than to be included in whatever we were doing, whether it be a walk in the woods, a ride in the boat, or an afternoon on the deck. After all, there's plenty to smell on a walk, plenty to see on a boat ride around the lake, and the deck-side bird feeders need to be protected from chipmunks and squirrels—in between naps.

Kaliber will have none of this. Her grandfather was imported from England, supposedly from the Queen's kennels, and royalty demands attention. An appropriate American term for her would be "High Maintenance." Even though she has reached Labrador middle age, she demands that fun things happen before a nap on the deck. Of course she hunts—pheasants, grouse, ducks, geese, chipmunks, mice—whatever is in season or happens to be available. But Wikipedia, despite its reputation, has her pegged—"As a breed (Labrador Retrievers), they are highly intelligent and capable of intense single-mindedness and focus if motivated or their interest is caught."

Intense single-mindedness? No stick is safe with Kal around. She will fetch the same piece of wood for an entire year without losing or tiring of it. Beyond that, she invents games for her own amusement when we tire of her unceasing begging to retrieve. That favorite stick, or maybe a tennis ball or a Frisbee, is carried to the end of the dock and nosed or paw-flipped into the lake. She whines at the sight of her precious toy in peril and then dives in head first to retrieve. A quick swim back to shore, a water-flinging, ear-flapping shake or two, and repeat over, and over, and over again.

Tonight, all the pent up energy of a late spring and the disappointment of being left at the cabin while I turkey-hunted, come together. It's as though that highly intelligent little mind behind the bright amber eyes realizes her springs are counted in people years, not doggie years. She demands to make the most of the handful left to her and pleads with me to play, whining and nudging me with her maple stick.

Frankly, I would rather sit back and relax. Crooked Lake calms to a blue sheet of glass in the last hour before dusk, mirroring the green reflections of the pines stepping up the slopes of the islands that are anchored to the right and left. The beavers, otters, and ducks are busy in a flurry of spring renewal, cutting ripples through the glass in the dim light. Mix in the yodeling of loons, with the hooting of the barred owls, and the occasional coyote choir. Add an almost total lack of manmade sound and it's easy to imagine this same scene playing out every spring since the glaciers retreated north ten thousand years ago.

Kal could care less about all this ambiance. She only wants to swim and fetch. I throw the heavy maple stick down the hill from the campfire, not just once, but time after time, splashing it out into the lake, breaking the once smooth surface. She chases, swims, and retrieves, time and time again.

When my arm can take no more, I throw once more. She spins away and chases. "Last one!" I yell after her. She knows what that means. She completes the retrieve and presents her precious hunk of maple to me one last time.

"Sweet," I tell her. She crashes back down the bank, ignoring the steps I labored over, and willingly plunges once more into water that was ice only last week. Back and forth, with no particular purpose in mind, she cruises the shore with stick in mouth. The big aluminum roll-in dock is still parked on shore but the small wooden one was left in all winter. She occasionally leaves the water, runs to the end of it, does the ritual shake, drops the stick in the water, and immediately jumps back in to retrieve.

As the evening passes, she checks back at the fire occasionally, dripping wet, tail happily wagging, carrying her stick. "Nice stick," I say. That's all the affirmation she needs. Back down the bank, splash into the lake, and resume swimming. Not a moment of a spring evening is to be wasted, even if I won't be a party to her silly games

The fire slowly burns down until its decision time. The smart thing to do would be to drown the fire and head back up the hill to the cabin in the fading light. Tomorrow's predawn wake up call for the morning turkey hunt isn't that far away. But I think I'll open one last beer, put another chunk of oak on the fire, and let this dog have her day. After all, it's spring.

Marsh Muirhead *Poetry*

NASCAR

Late on a Sunday afternoon in winter,
the failures and excesses of the weekend
tallied and countered with naps and aspirin,
brief efforts at reading *The New York Times*,
a bowl of Ben and Jerry's Chunky Monkey,
I hit the remote for another session
of channel surfing, find NASCAR
Live from Daytona!
bright sunshine and the roar of engines—
the billboards of our desires
at a hundred and ninety miles an hour,
around and around and around
until somebody spins, hits the wall,
smoke and debris filling the screen,
the car flipping over and over,
shedding its tires, spilling the beans,
M&Ms, Gatorade, Bud Light, Viagra—
before coming to rest, a steaming heap.
The driver emerges from the carnage,
waving to the crowd and cameras.
When the microphone arrives
he thanks his pit crew, the many sponsors,
his wife and, finally, the fans in the stands
who roar their approval as the race resumes—
other heroes carrying the flag
for country and corporation—
risking it all in the wildness of speed,
going like hell, if only in mad circles.

Deanna Perchyshyn *Fiction*

The Last Bus Ride

Jeni's bus came to a halt as she pulled on her hood and stepped outside. The building was lit up and waiting for her, every third Thursday. Here again. What happened to all the other Thursdays?

If you didn't know what was inside, you might say it was beautiful. The crumbling stone wall could be protecting a king and queen inside their castle. The bus driver waved and smiled at her as she stepped off the bus. She pretended not to see.

She walked away, avoiding the mud puddles. Even foggy, rainy air felt nice after being inside all day. All her life really. She didn't want to come. She didn't need to come, but she "had to." It was family obligation for somebody who didn't deserve it.

They were back, but they left her alone now. After twenty-one years, they should. How many times could you say no to an interview? A new trial could start the media circus again. But it would prove nothing. He confessed, nearly boasted. She remembered how the town doubled in size. Would the reporters come back? There had been a million tragedies since.

After she rang the buzzer, the guard let her in. He scanned her purse, gave her the pitying look. His bald head shone under the bright lights.

"I'll get him. Have a seat, ma'am."

It was always ma'am. No one called her Jeni. Miss Plitski to the children at school. They never hugged her like they did the other teachers. Once in sixteen years, a new girl named Clara hugged her. No more hugs once she found out. Somehow, she was guilty by bloodline.

He ushered her inside the visitor's room. At the middle table, behind the glass, she set the pan of brownies underneath her chair. *You're lucky to have a job. There's nowhere else to go. The story follows you. The house is paid for.* Still, she dreamed of escaping.

Dad was the fortunate one. He died without knowing. There was no cruelty, but there was always speculation. Mom wanted the best for Jeni and William too. A broken heart made for an early descent to her grave.

William came to the window. He smiled. He was scruffy. Usually he shaved, but his hours are numbered. Is he counting minutes?

"Hi, Jeni," he said. He forced nice, his tone condescending.

"Hello, William. How are you?"

"Alive. Still eating rotten food."

"You look well."

"No treats for your brother?'

"I've been busy. Papers. Conferences. You know."

"I don't know. I would have liked one more of your brownies before my . . . punishment."

He stared at her sullenly, his eyes burning into hers. "Are you coming?"

She was silent. She knows what he is asking. Without the scruff, he is a handsome man. He protected her at school, shared his lunch. He taught her how to play chess. She was not an even match for him, but a competitor still. William went to college and ran a bank. It didn't seem to satisfy him.

"Have you asked for forgiveness?"

"Asked who?" he replied smugly.

"God."

"Can't really see the point."

"Mother would have liked you to ask," she said, eyes downward. Jeni looked up at him. It had been like this before, but now he is so obvious, unrepentant.

"You're probably right."

"Pray. Ask the chaplain to bless you," she said. "God forgives everyone who truly repents."

"I'm not sorry."

She shook her head, holding back tears. She'll give the brownies to someone else.

"I'm not coming," she blurted.

"You're my sister!" he said, finally showing emotion.

"I couldn't get the day off work," she said.

"No wonder you've never had a man. You're all bones and bossiness, like a little girl."

"I'll pray for you."

He scowled, got up and exited the room, without turning back. A tear dropped but she wiped it away with her hand and forced herself to remain stoic, unemotional. *I just need to get home*, she thought.

It was dark when she walked the long sidewalk to the bus stop. *I am free*, she thinks. There are no more third Thursdays.

She moved more quickly now, thought of skipping. The bus was there already. Then she slowed. *I am already dead. Somewhere in between the murders and the conviction, I died. It is always Thursday.*

Jeni stepped on the bus and handed the driver the pan of brownies.

"Thank you. What's the occasion?"

"They were . . . never mind." She shrugged.

No one else was on the bus. He smiled at her again; she didn't reciprocate. She took a seat in the second row. The dizziness she felt made the walk to the back of the bus too far. She stared out the window as they rolled along, seeing the colorful houses teeming with life, normalcy.

"I'm working a double today," he volunteered. "My friend wanted the day off. I'm Sam. Sam Finley."

The name is familiar.

"I'm Jeni. Jeni Plitski."

"I know who you are."

She looked at him curiously. They were silent for a few miles, the silence nearly suffocating her. She peeked at Sam, noticed his blondish red hair. He was early into his midlife, looked friendly from his side profile.

"It's a small community. There's nowhere to hide," he said.

She gulped, felt ashamed. The redness crept into her cheeks. She could see herself in the window.

"You grew up here?" she asked.

"No."

"How long have you lived here?"

"Long enough to have driven you out to that prison once a month for many years."

She looked at the floor.

"This is my stop," she said.

"I know."

Jeni stood and walked to the front, waited.

"I don't blame you," he said.

"Excuse me?"

"My niece. She was one of his victims," he said.

"I'm so sorry. After his—"

"Next Wednesday, I know. I've been waiting."

"I hope you have some peace. Some closure," she said.

The bus stopped but Sam didn't open the door. Jeni waited.

"I came for her funeral, over eighteen years ago. I couldn't leave my sister. She's alone . . . her husband left. They both blamed themselves."

The tears started again. "May I get out?"

"Of course. I'm not trying to hold you captive. Could I call you sometime?"

"Why? I can't bring her back. I wish—there were six women. We had no idea."

"That's not why. I think you're . . . lovely," he confessed.

Sam combed his hair with his fingers. Jeni noticed his rugged features, his pleasant face.

"I just want to talk. Take you out somewhere. I've admired you all these years. Not many people would keep going. You're number seven."

"What?" she asked.

"His seventh victim. Haven't you punished yourself long enough? Haven't we all?"

Sam opened the door.

"If this is some sort of twisted joke, please leave me alone."

He shook his head.

"You can reach me at school."

A few steps from the bus, Jeni pulled out her ponytail and let her hair fall, years' worth of growth. She began the short hike to the house where she grew up with her family and where she lives now, alone. A house once full of life. *It's time for a haircut,* she thought as she heard Sam drive away, into the thick of fog and darkness of night.

Larry Ellingson *Poetry*

Spring Plowing

This bony old man,
stick leaning, three-legged man,
hat and gloves on a warm day
gazing at his rusted plow.

Fields ready to turn.
Recalling, dreaming,
when he was strong and strapping.

Hitch plow to tractor
drop the blades and pull
north then south
cutting the black earth open
releasing the sweet musk.

The smell of fresh furrows arouse
and he recalls his young wife
and soft sweet lips and the
soft sweet penetration
as though warmed by the sun
that will never come again.
Oh! that hard sweet rusted plow!

Cindy Fox *Fiction*

Breaking Out

Six months of incarceration is a long time for anyone, especially for a country gal like me. I knew I had to get out, away from the rank air of yesterday's meals of fried onions and northern pike, to yank free from my sweatshirt splattered with bacon grease that isn't worth changing because when you're confined in close quarters, every thing and every one smells the same.

Straddling the garbage container between my knees, I hoist up the bag. A whoosh of rotten things—chicken bones, orange peelings, moldy bread, and unopened junk mail—is snuffed out with a tight tug of the drawstrings, double-knotted for good measure. I stop at the dump and, for the first time this year, I drive to my cabin on the Otter Tail River.

Spring arrived on the calendar weeks ago, but winter keeps lifting up its snotty nose. Last week was unseasonably warm, but today, I step out of the car and winter's cold breath slaps me in the face. I pull up my collar, crossing my arms to snuggle my hands in my armpits, and walk head pointed down to plow into the blustery wind.

As I inspect the aftereffects of winter, the mushy ground sucks the shoes off my feet. The lawn is suffering from a hangover and is still asleep. The matted grass is littered with candy wrappers, drink straws, and cigarette butts. The yard looks like WE Fest the morning after. I pick up a weather-beaten shingle, ragged with claw marks after losing its grip flapping in gale force winds. I write *check cabin roof* on my spring project list.

I watch the river snake-dancing through the beaten marsh like some courtship ritual when a head bobs up from the water. Greasy brown hair, slicked back, this guy is my worst enemy. He nose dives and his tail smacks the water like *I* was the intruder. Up the river bank, three limbs of my cherry tree lay strewn near the edge, teeth marks on their pencil-pointed ends a dead giveaway to the beaver's shenanigans. Leave it to beaver to prune my trees.

My cabin builder's right hand man built my deck steps in an afternoon, no doubt while drinking beer with his other hand. The steps he crafted from half-split logs are so unsafe only a toddler can use them. Did he think we liked to step sideways to get on and off the deck? I test a step and it sags under my weight, the untreated logs bloated with water that drips off the roof. The once-green moss that grows where no one dares to tread is now brown with tints of gold. I add *steps* to my list.

I groan and a shiver runs down my spine when I survey the south side of the cabin. The guaranteed-for-life log sealant is flaking off and the chinking no longer feels a close bond to the logs either. The paint on the window trim is cracked and peeling like my chapped lips. Although my cabin passed its physical exam last fall, it now needs major surgery. I envision my summer guests tubing down the lazy river while my hands are chained to a paintbrush and a caulking gun in the hot sun. I add *help* to my growing list.

Back in the car, I drive eight miles to purchase screws to fix a sagging gutter that has dribbled snow melt into a treacherous ice mound on my front steps, a liability claim waiting to happen. I enter the hardware store and catch a whiff of oil, paint, wood and metal—simple, sensible smells.

I'm greeted by Mark, his Fleet Supply pocket protector crammed with pens and miniature screwdrivers. "Hey, long time no see. Are you enjoying our brisk spring weather?"

"Brisk isn't the word for it," I say as I eyeball the clearance bin of woolen caps and mittens.

He takes the screw I chiseled off my steps. Rolling it in his leathery fingers, he says, "That's a 7/8 inch gutter screw."

I follow his small-town unhurried gait through the gardening aisle, past hoes and rakes. In the back of the store we reach a soup-to-nuts collection of screws, meticulously sorted in bins against the wall. He drops the screws in my hand, but before I can ask if he knows a reliable handyman, he is gone. Not walking. He is running alongside a young man whose green-speckled face tells me there's a mishap in the paint mixing aisle.

I browse through the store but don't see anything I need, not right now anyway. Clutching five screws, I feel like a cheapskate at the checkout line. The cashier rings up $3.85.

I hand her $4.00, and ask, "How is business?"

Staring at my screws, she says, "Not too good."

I grimace, leaving my 15 cents on the counter.

Back at the cabin, I sit in my car and need a reason to dillydally. I stare at my ice-capped steps and remember the mountain of Ice Melt bags piled by the hardware store's entrance. A friendly reminder I walked past not once, but twice, I now face the risk of breaking my back.

I'm hitting my head against the steering wheel when I hear a whining noise like a distant chainsaw. A mosquito mindlessly bumps against my windshield. Like any Minnesotan, my first instinct is to squish it, but instead I pause for a moment, and then crack open the window.

Sonja Kosler *Poetry*

At the End of the Dock

A waning half moon
is suspended
in a slow-motion
vanishing act.
My legs sway lazy arcs
toes blend lunar light
into drowsy midnight lake.

Breathe basswood, balsam,
fish-scented air.

Solitary loon
drifts, dips, dives.
She emerges near the dock.
raises up, flaps her wings,
settles back to drifting.
Moonlight path ripples
with her motion,
then straightens, calms.

Is her life beginning or
closer to the end?

I lift callused feet
from lake water.
Drips tick toward a tomorrow
arriving too soon.

Kathryn Kirmis Medellin *Fiction*

The Chance Encounter

"We will begin boarding American Flight 368 going to Boston. All first class passengers and those who need assistance may board at this time. Please have your boarding passes ready."

Maggie Sterling, limping and using a cane, proceeded to get in line. Once on the plane she found her aisle seat, stowed her small carry-on beneath the seat in front of her and sat down. Maggie hoped there would be no more passengers in her row but, three minutes before the door closed, a couple claimed the two empty seats.

She laid her head back and closed her eyes. Her visit to Florida had been a pleasant winter break with daughter, Teri, and her lively family. Now, she was eager to get back to her own little home in New Bedford, Massachusetts.

"Would you like to move to the first class section?" said a hushed voice. Was someone talking to her?

Maggie opened her eyes. An airline attendant was bending down asking her if she would like to move to the first class section.

"We noticed you were limping and using a cane. We have two empty seats. You would be more comfortable where there is more room, and it won't add anything to your fare."

Maggie thought, "A cane, a limp, and a short, white-haired, little old lady." She wouldn't tell him she sprained her ankle playing dodge ball with her six-year-old grandson.

"I've never flown first class. What a kind offer," Maggie replied as she unbuckled her seatbelt. Dan, the attendant, carried her bag to the front of the plane and seated her in the last of the four rows. A perfect place for Maggie. She had a good view of the forward cabin.

"Would you care for a drink?" Dan asked. "We have wine, soft drinks, tea or coffee."

"Oh, a cup of coffee would be nice."

Maggie could hardly believe her good fortune. Wait until she told her family about her flight in first class.

As she was drinking the coffee, she looked around. The backs of the seats were too high to see over, but she could see between them. Two gentlemen in business suits were in front of her. Across the aisle from them was a man wearing jeans and a sport coat with a young woman sitting beside him. She wondered if they were married. Her family said she never let her mind rest. She had been curious since she was born. Anyway, that is what her father always said.

Directly across the aisle from Maggie was an elderly man with a white mustache, a bulbous nose and a belly to match. His heavy white eyebrows reminded her of the preacher in her church when she was a little girl. She couldn't see the person sitting next to him; he was obscured by the preacher. Four people sat in the front seats out of her view.

After lunch, served on a china plate with a linen napkin, Maggie laid her head back and slept. She was awakened by the intercom announcement that the flight would reach their destination in about an hour. It was then she noticed the person in a front seat. The passenger had turned her head to talk to Dan as he handed her a drink. Maggie sat straight up and bent forward. Where had she seen that woman? And then she remembered.

Thirty years ago, when she was dining at the Peninsula Hotel in Hong Kong, a young lady walked into the restaurant. Everyone turned to look at her. She was elegant. Maggie had traveled in many different areas of the world, and had been an ardent people watcher. She had never seen anyone so beautiful. No wonder heads turned.

"Everyone notices Tanya," Maggie's waiter said. "She is a White Russian. Many White Russians came to China during and after the Russian Civil War. Tanya comes here often and alone. Many of the women are attractive but there is no one like Tanya," he said as he walked away, stumbling into the table next to Maggie.

Dan was not talking to Tanya or at least the Tanya Maggie had seen so many years ago. It was shocking to see someone who resembled that elegant person in Hong Kong. Maggie studied her; she was so similar to Tanya. As she raised her right hand Maggie's attention was drawn to the exquisite rings on her fingers. No wonder she was in first class.

Maggie knew her jewels. In her early twenties she had worked for her Uncle Magnus Beckman, whose reputation for his knowledge about gems was worldwide. The rings she saw on the passenger's hand were some of the best—even at this distance she could tell. A diamond ring and an amber ring. Maggie was partial to amber. This one was very striking in a gold setting.

"I've always wanted an amber ring that beautiful," she sighed.

Maggie noticed a luggage tag on the carry-on under the passenger's seat—Liza Simonov, Alexander Hotel, Granite Falls, Massachusetts.

When the plane door opened, Dan escorted Maggie to the door and, as she departed, she turned to him and said, "Thank you ever so much for your kindness."

She smiled as she limped onto the ramp leaning heavily on her cane.

Two weeks after Maggie returned home, she was in line for a teller at the New Bedford Bank. It was a snowy winter afternoon, and the people were dressed for the weather: scarves, gloves and coats with hoods pulled over their heads. The customer at the teller's window was wearing a red winter jacket with a fur-trimmed hood. Her purse was on the counter.

Maggie was becoming impatient. She was third in line, it was late, and she was anxious to return home as she watched the wind whipping the snow around near the window where she stood.

"What a large purse that woman has," Maggie thought. As that thought crossed Maggie's mind, the customer hurriedly turned away from the teller's window and ran out the door, dropping one of her gloves. It fell on the floor near Maggie. She picked it up, ready to go after the fleeing customer.

"I have just been robbed!" the teller screamed, throwing her hands in the air. "It was that lady with the big purse. She had a gun. She robbed me before I could press the alarm button!"

In what seemed like two seconds, three bank guards arrived and ushered the startled customers out of the bank. The wind had increased, blowing the falling snow into little drifts. Maggie was glad to get home after the exciting afternoon.

When she finally settled into her easy chair, she remembered the glove. What would she do with one glove? She took it out of her jacket pocket; something dropped and rolled under her chair. She knelt down on her hands and knees and retrieved the object. She would make a phone call in the morning.

Two days after the robbery, Maggie picked up the *New Bedford Times* from her front stoop, sat at her kitchen table with her morning coffee, and read the headlines on the front page:

NEW BEDFORD BANK ROBBERY SOLVED

An anonymous phone call to the New Bedford police led them to the person who robbed the local bank two days ago. The police arrested Liza Simonov and her two accomplices at the Alexander Hotel in Granite Falls. The arrest solves several jewel and bank robberies that have taken place along the East Coast this year—the story went on.

Maggie put the newspaper down, looked at the ring finger on her right hand. Liza Simonov would have no need for the amber ring in the gold setting where she was going.

Winter Night

Gnarled shadows of oak branches
reach like arthritic fingers across the snow.

Bitter cold grasps the night
under a glaring December moon.

Pines stand stoic, sentinels of the woods,
bound by snow, unable to stir.

Footsteps sink deep, erased by pine I pull.
Suspended puffs of breath linger.

From my cabin window a warm light beckons.

Peggy Trojan *Poetry Editor's Choice*

giving it up

cows
raising chickens
canning tomatoes
traveling abroad
fishing in Alaska
feeding birds in winter
canoeing upstream to fish
walking four miles a day
cross country skiing
deer hunting
wife of sixty-nine years
cooking for company
computer correspondence
golf
exercises on the floor
picking raspberries
lifting weights in a chair
driving
baking bread
walking
making it to a hundred
asking to come home
everything

Sharon Harris *Creative Nonfiction*

The Old Homestead

I have gone back to see the old home place. The farm house has paint peeling on the outside walls; the screen door is ajar. The attached woodshed is still full of firewood. A leaning garage is nearby and also the big barn that still touches the sky, now with broken windows gaping.

Inside the house, the faded linoleum is buckled. The ceiling paint is cracked and puckered from leaks. There is a sad mustiness in the air hanging over everything.

I walk through the rooms, happy to review past memories but sad to see the changes. I step out onto the screened-in porch. Here the dust from the dirt road coats every single thing. This porch used to reach around two sides of the house—now only a small portion of it remains. The rest of the porch was enclosed when another bedroom, a laundry room and a new stairway to the basement were needed.

My steps take me back through the house now, looking at the shapes of the rooms, recalling the way it must have looked. The current kitchen was once tiny. There was a different bedroom that was changed to make the kitchen larger; a bathroom was also carved out of the space.

If I look closely, I can see all the edges of the old house, the shapes of the first rooms, the remains of the original homestead, the hopes and dreams of the first builders as they started a life here on the prairie.

Audrey Kletscher Helbling *Poetry*

The Farmer's Song

Out of rote he follows the path from house to barn,
from barn to shed, steel-toed boots beating a rhythm
upon the earth, into this land which claims his soul.

He reaches for the paint-chipped handle,
his grease-stained fingers connecting with worn metal
like hammer to nail in the movements of his day.

Farming defines the lyrics of his life written upon hands
that have measured yields, directed tractors, pitched manure,
stroked calves, performed seasons of backbreaking labor.

Inside the shed, as he latches wrench to bolt,
he ponders the final verses of his years, the songs he'll sing
when age frays his memory, grips his hands in a hallelujah chorus.

Kevin Zepper *Fiction*

Neighborly

Yes, it is a beautiful neighborhood. The Noland place next door is a real find. Lots of trees, shrubs, and green grass. Maybe it's because of this being the dead end and all. Lived in this house for fifty years this April. The wife passed in '85 but I just couldn't leave this old house. Too many memories here to just up and leave, retire to the Wakeville Old Folks Home, you know? Too many birthdays, Yules, Halloweens, and, March 7—can't forget that.

Over there? Across the street? Yes, someone still lives there. That's Dorothy. Dorothy Brisbane. Been my neighbor for the past thirty years. I know it looks deserted but she's still alive and kicking. Yard's like a damn forest, though. Been like that since she moved in. Suppose it isn't that mangy when you get used to it. Kind of makes you feel like you're out in the country really.

Yeah, I said March 7. Tomorrow I know that old Dorothy is gonna howl. Figured that you might as well know what you're getting into here. I swear I ain't no loony either! Yeah, I mean howl, like a lonely north wind, enough to make the dead shake in their graves.

You see it all started about ten years back. Dorothy goes and a-dopts this wild pup. The critter was in tough shape at first. Looked like it got into some kind of scrap with a mower or one of those new weed-whackers. Well, Dorothy nursed that pup back to health, quick as Charlie. She named it "Ghost" because it was silver-gray in color.

Dorothy asked the local vet about the critter, what kind of pooch it was. She comes to find that the dog is part wolf, an honest to god timber wolf. Most of the genuine articles are farther north, up near the iron range. Didn't really seem to shock her too much. Ghost was a fine animal, really.

Well, she gets to loving and enjoying the company of Ghost a lot. Wherever she went, Ghost wasn't too far behind her. You ever have a dog? See, you know what that's like. A spaniel? They're great with kids. I had a mutt named Mook. You really get attached to a dog, no bones about that. Almost like you have this bond with them, like family.

It wasn't too long after Ghost was around that I began to wake up in the middle of the night. I'd hear this chilling howl. Hey, I thought, it had to be Ghost. No other critters in the neighborhood. Just getting used to it till I heard a second howl joining with the first.

Now I know you must think I'm off my nut but I wouldn't shuck you on that. It was down right frosty. Those two howls together, like two soft steam whistles in a fog. Went through me like December sleet. Me? No, I didn't complain, call the cops, nothing like that. There are so few of us on the block and I didn't want to cause problems for the old gal. After losing her hubby Roy years back and that stint at Wakeville State Hospital, I felt for her. Still can't get that sound out of my head, mind you.

Well then, here comes March 7. It was early in the morning, about five or so. I heard this shriek coming from across the street near Dorothy's house. I got up and ran over to her place to see what was the matter. It was terrible. Something had gotten hold of Ghost. That pooch must have been run over in the middle of the night. I could see the red wet patches across Dorothy's over-grown lawn where the grass was matted down. Ghost was by the porch. Must have been dead a couple of hours.

I can't describe the look on the old gal's face. It was flat blank. Her eyes were dilated and glazed over. She'd mumble Roy's name, then Ghost's. Real sad. It's hard to forget something like that.

Well, I did call the police. I had to. Didn't know what to do. Might have hurt herself or something. They kept her in the clink for a couple of days. She was good, didn't give them any trouble. They destroyed what was left of Ghost at the shelter while she was in the pokey. I know that she would have wanted Ghost buried next to Roy. They got laws against that sort of thing though, you know?

I checked up on her a couple of times. She was polite, quiet and all, but I didn't see her too much after that. She kept inside a lot, blocked her windows up with cardboard and aluminum foil. It was as if she was denying all light and life after that.

I know that date, though. Five years ago Ghost died. On that cool, damp night every year since, I hear the baying of a wolf from across the way, like some sad critter pining for its dead pup.

Sorry I got off on that spiel there. Don't see too many folks so I get to talking. I think you'll like the Noland place next door. Good place to raise your kids, raise a family, lots of green and trees. Come to think of it, have I told you about the Atwood place just down the block?

Peggy Trojan *Poetry Honorable Mention*

Photograph

Posed in the yard
Sophie, sitting, holding baby Ellen
husband Victor standing
wearing his suit jacket and good hat,
hand on Wayne's shoulder.

My father, age four,
shirt buttoned to the neck
hair slicked, pants safety-pinned,
hiding a little behind his mother's arm.
He looks intently into the camera lens
to what's coming.
Past losing his right eye when he is ten
past the 1918 Hinckley fire
that takes their house and cows
and burns his pet ram black,
into that most terrible part
where his dad dies
leaving all eight of them and Sophie
on the farm with no aid or money.
He is already sad.

He can't see just a little farther.
Far enough to see me
standing on the porch, waving.

Selling my Soul

That's what it felt like
the day we put the house up for sale.
Dad's possessions gone—
to us kids, Goodwill, the dump.
We cleaned, called the Realtor, signed the listing.
I couldn't drive by anymore. The "For Sale"
post in the driveway hurt to look at,
felt like an ugly sliver was lodged in my chest.
It wasn't on the market long;
the Realtor reported numerous showings,
good comments, praised the ever-lauded
location, location, location.
Once a purchase agreement was in place
it took mere weeks for title work,
inspections, and a scheduled closing.
The night before the transfer
I drove to the house, let myself in with the key
I'd soon hand over to a stranger,
and walked through the rooms alone.
Would they love the kitchen, make roast beef
on Sundays, bake cookies, play rummy at the table?
Would they close the bathroom door,
crank up the furnace and get the bathroom hot
before their shower on a cold winter day?
I wondered if they'd watch sitcoms in the living room,
where they'd put the Christmas tree.
Would their daughter sneak out the basement door

to meet a boyfriend down the road
where he'd parked his car, headlights off?
Would they have a dog, maybe a multi-colored mutt,
who'd sprawl across the front porch and bark at strangers
but wag his tail at the same time?
I packed the million memories, carried them with me
out the door I'd never walk through again.

Adrian S. Potter *Fiction Honorable Mention*

An Annotated Version of Hell

For a bunch of crappy reasons too complicated to explain, I cram a handful of Xanax in my mouth and wash them down with cheap beer. Although I hope everything will happen instantaneously, it doesn't feel like the pills are going to kill me. Considering my uncanny ability to screw up simple tasks, the bungling of an impromptu suicide attempt wouldn't be considered a surprise.

What is a surprise is how relaxed I feel. Here I am, content to remain face up on the hardwood floor of my apartment, blinking deliberately and tapping my teeth against the numb lump of tongue in my mouth. Lukewarm sweat stains my T-shirt and drips down my forehead. My skin tingles as consciousness slips away. And then without warning it comes: a shrill, powerful ring. The sound slaps me so hard that I imagine stars orbiting my head, similar to the ones a dumbfounded cartoon character sees after an unfortunate thump to the skull.

Drowsy and surprised, I simply lay still. Drool drips onto my whiskers as time slows from its usual sober pace. Outside the window is a busy avenue, so I watch the headlights of evening traffic on the glass. Another ring. Its echo ricochets inside my cranium.

I shift my body. One more booming ring. I finally realize it's the telephone, a fact I would've discerned immediately if my thoughts were lucid. I glare at the phone, a cordless Walmart special perched on a nearby coffee table. Who would dial up a dying man? Since when did phones ring in the residences of losers overdosing on prescription pills? Whoever is calling—a truant lover, a belligerent boss, or an irate bill collector—probably has a hunch that I'm falling just short of terminating my hapless life. They know I can't even do that simple task right.

At this moment, I realize that I desperately want to live—a fatal case of buyer's remorse. I lunge for the phone. But the drugs and booze have made my muscles feeble, my balance unsteady, and my concentration wane. No matter how hard I try, the receiver remains inches from my grasp.

Then I begin to entertain the idea that perhaps I'm already dead. Maybe this apartment is hell and everything is exactly the same in hell as it is on earth, except sometimes I get phone calls that I actually want to answer. The person on the other end could be someone who might save me, but I'm destined to never reach the handset and receive salvation. The phone just continues ringing, and I fail to pick it up. Instead I am doomed to lay here, with nothing to do but contemplate my mistakes for what feels like eternity.

Waiting for Yowzah

It was 1939 and life was good. At eight years of age, I was the oldest kid on the block, if you don't count my older sister who wasn't really on the block that much. Gary Crowe, a neighbor kid who was a mere 7 1/2, was my best pal. The two of us hung out together after school doing kid stuff like jacks, hop-scotch, kick-the-can, and playing mumbletypeg with a rusty old jackknife. That and waiting for Yowzah, the ice man.

Home refrigerators were still a luxury in 1939. We had one in our house, a Leonard. The evaporator coil on top kept the little room behind our kitchen warm and moist, much to the delight of the resident mold spores. The tiny freezer box inside the refrigerator was just large enough to hold two ice cube trays or a quart of ice cream. My favorite flavor was Butter Brickle. When that was all gone, I could go back to having an ice cube in my root beer.

With such a magical appliance right there in the house, our family no longer needed to buy ice. Nearly half the people on our block still had iceboxes though, including Gary's folks. His dad was the local distributor for Cho-Chos, which were ice cream bars sold in grocery stores. Needless to say, leftover Cho-Cho samples brought home had to be eaten quickly or they'd melt. Gary and I, chocolate goo dripping off our elbows, were always happy to oblige.

Tuesdays and Fridays were the ice man days. You could hear the big flatbed ice truck coming before you could see it. Then there it was, rounding the corner and roaring onto our block. Whatever Gary and I were doing, we'd quit on the spot and turn to watch the bearded old driver scan the houses, looking for customers. If people needed ice they would put a large orange-and-black pasteboard sign in a front window, tilted so that the proper numeral—25, 50, 75 or 100—was on top. That's how the ice man knew how many pounds of ice they needed.

As soon as the truck stopped at the first house, the two of us would run up and ask the driver if we could ride along. Winking and grinning at us so his nonexistent front teeth showed, he would growl, "Yowzah!" He rarely said anything else, so that is what we named him. With permission granted, Gary and I would each climb up on a front fender, straddle an attached headlight, and ride down the street like kings to the next window sign.

When Yowzah had finished chiseling a 100-pound block of ice down to the right size (the regulars rarely needed a whole 100 pounds), he would tong the block onto his shoulder and carry it up to the house. That's when Gary and I would hop down, race to the back of the truck and begin popping ice chips into our hot little mouths. Heaven! When my mom heard about this, she sighed and said she guessed the germs were too cold to kill me.

This routine was repeated, gloriously, until the truck reached the street corner and we relinquished our thrones, crunching ice with our existent teeth and shouting "Bye!" With a wave and a "Yowzah!" the driver gunned the ice truck around the corner, our kingdom gone until the next ice day. In our opinion that odd expression of his was an immigrant's attempt to pronounce "Yes, sir" through gaps in his teeth, a term of respect we boys were all too happy to accept. If, instead, "Yowzah" was Polish for "Beat it, kid," we'd rather not know.

How Did They Know it was Us?

We tossed them off the high haystack
in Charlie Strait's field;
we'd play there
when the bull was in the far pasture.

Four boys, my older brother and I
and a couple of neighbors,
playing with matches.
Maybe they were comets

or shooting stars
more likely Kamikazes or MIGs
shot down mid-flight
before they could do damage.

The stack started to smolder,
our hearts filled our throats
as we tumbled down the side.
We tried to smother it, stamp it out.

We were too late, so we ran.
Someone called it in, I suppose
a neighbor. The fire trucks raced by
to end the fire's spread.

The neighborhood gathered
to watch the action
except four boys casually
building castles in a sandbox.

Ronald J. Palmer *Poetry*

The Retired Ref On A Walk

It's morning. I walk along an old football field and spot
just beyond the end zone a number of geese standing as if
choosing sides for a game.

(No clue where there was a football.)

Cars on the street pass me
the exhaust as harsh as angry fans
I cannot throw a flag;
I think of players who have ignored warnings.

Looking back at the field, maybe
the geese are getting ready to honk in formation
and march a half-time show. I don't know. I am just glad to
see that the animal kingdom can find
a use for what is left behind.

Helen Hansen *Creative Nonfiction*

My First Hunting Season

Fall has come to northern Minnesota, but soon winter will chase it away because she is already playing quietly in the wind. My dad and I walk on the dewy grass. We're dressed in layers for warmth and covered in orange to follow the hunting season rules. We climb into the stand and open three windows with the fourth closed at our backs. To my left and my front I see trails cutting through the trees, and to my right I see my father's hay field with the pasture flowing out of it.

I close my eyes and feel the morning. The air chills my cheek, and I feel the warmth of the sun as it creeps up against my skin. I open my eyes to see the sky is clear and blue. The forest wakes for the day, even though the sun has yet to fully rise. Squirrels run through the trees and brush, and birds chirp to greet the morning. I see steam rise from the surface of the waterhole that rests in the middle of the pasture. It's getting colder, and soon the waterhole will freeze, chasing away the warmth it has held. This day is perfect for hunting.

I glance away, needing to focus, but it's hard. I'm nervous and excited because today is my first time hunting. I pray I won't miss. I look at Dad and he smiles. I smile back knowing it would make him proud to see his only daughter kill a deer.

I look out to the field and see shadows cast by trees. They stretch across the field, trying to engulf it before the sun chases them away. A light fog covers the dew that rests on the hay. I look to the trail in front of me, and see the sun peeking through the leaves that remain on the trees.

I feel Dad poke my side to quietly get my attention. I look at him and he points below the stand. Beneath us is a spike buck. I lift my gun, but Dad shakes his head and mouths "too close." I lower my gun, and watch him disappear out of my line of sight. He walks slowly, carefully picking his way across the tall grass and bushes. He stalks the woods, keeping his head level with his body, trying to find his prey whether it be food or doe. His sound slowly disappears as he continues through the brush. I focus back on the trail ahead of me waiting for my chance.

I feel Dad poke me again and look to see him pointing at the field. I follow his out-stretched arm, and see a doe emerge from the woods. Her head is held high and her feet rise high off the ground as she walks. She gazes slowly across the field, like a queen gazing across her kingdom.

Out of the corner of my eye I see Dad nod, and I slowly raise my gun. The doe stops and stares at the pasture as I rest the butt of my rifle against my shoulder. My breath is shaky when Dad whispers something in my ear that I don't understand. I feel my hands sweat as I look through the scope and find my crosshairs. I place them behind her shoulder, knowing it will be the killing shot. I release the safety, take a deep breath, and count to three.

Nothing happens, and I have to let out my breath. She turns away from me and walks. I replace the safety as Dad silently curses, and then tells me to stay ready. The doe moves slowly, swinging her hips like a girl would tease a boy. She stops again and turns to the pasture.

Dad whispers, "You can still take her. Aim slightly above her body so the bullet will angle down when you fire to still hit the kill zone."

My breathing is shakier than before as I look through the scope to find my crosshairs again. I place them just above her shoulders, release the safety, take a deep breath, and count to three.

Nothing, again nothing happens. The doe turns to the woods with her head held high, and slowly disappears into its depths alive. I replace the safety, silently curse myself, and lower my gun. Dad sighs heavily, and shakes his head.

"I'm not mad, but you had a perfect shot. Why didn't you shoot her?" he asks.

"I don't know," I reply.

"Would you have shot the buck?"

"Yes," is my immediate response.

As silence engulfs the stand, I keep seeing the doe walking into the woods alive. I just can't believe I didn't pull the trigger. I freeze. No, I couldn't pull the trigger. I couldn't shoot that doe, nor would I have shot that buck. I can't explain why, not to Dad and not to myself. I feel tears gathering at the back of my eyes, and look away from Dad knowing I won't hunt with him again.

Laura L. Hansen *Poetry*

First Steps

—For Caitlin

This afternoon my son read his first book ever,
his sticky baby fingers grasping the corners like suction cups;
his lips bubble with saliva as he made the truck go *vroom.*

This day my son fixed his attention on the black shapes
of words, the twisted shells of the numbers,
and counted one-two-four.

My son—today, this hour—took his palm
and placed it on the blue truck, the red car, held
for the first time the spine of language.

Together we count the four wheels, alone he finds
the hidden box, lifts the flap that opens the truck's door.
Together we travel the road of words, flying

along the printed page like bees, gobbling up
white space like hungry ants on fresh-baked bread.
My son reads today for the first time,

he reads and takes
his first   hesitant   steps   away from me.

Marlys Guimaraes *Creative Nonfiction*

Sin in a Small Package

Sunday-best shoes swing back and forth in the pew, keeping time to the children's song—*1-2-3 the devil's after me, 4-5-6 he's always throwing sticks, 7-8-9 he misses all the time.* After that, we sing about being careful what you see or hear or say because the Father up above is looking.

My daddy's sermons were filled with blazing fires and pictures of big thrones and an angry man in a white robe with a long finger pointing —straight at me. I knew I was being chased by the devil and no matter how careful I was, I would eventually see or hear something I shouldn't and end up in that fire—forever.

Mama's hands floated over black and white keys, Daddy's voice boomed, leading the group that assembled for worship. My brother and I wiggled and squirmed on the front pew. We played finger games, squeezing off the circulation to each other's hand until it got numb and blue just to let go and watch color return.

Sweat rings on white shirts mingled with Evening in Paris perfume, skirts stuck to damp thighs, and long neckties cried to be loosened.

It happened on that hot day. It was between services. I was naughty in church. A long arm grabbed me and carried me outside. The voice wasn't his ministerial voice, but the voice of my angry father, a voice I feared. On the front lawn of the church, he bent me over his knee and started spanking.

I didn't mean to, but I let go. I peed. The spanking stopped. "Oh no," he cried as he looked down at his wet suit pants and ran into the house to change clothes before starting the next service.

Power. Oh the sweetness of power. It surged through me. I was saved.

Cheryl Weibye Wilke *Poetry*

New Shoes, 1965

My father fit new shoes on small town
and country families. Rand patent leather for the girls.
Buster Brown's iron-clad oxfords for the boys.

For the lady in her floral crepe Sunday dress, he had Stride
Rite's bow pump set on a modest heel. And hefty Star
Brand boots for the men unchanged from stall to aisle.

In the same way he sized up feet, he watched his young
daughter fill the empty back-acre with wild saplings dug
from the neighbor's woods, and fill her bedroom walls

with dime store posters of untamed mustangs. She
wore Poll-Parrot shoes with straps and heel taps that clicked
like ponies upon canyon floors. She was one of two

town girls who strode her horse up and down the forests
of Main Street. In the same quiet way
he replaced each fading tree with an oak or maple,

he sized up feet and fit new shoes.

The Secret

Outside, snow falls like ticker tape on the Canyon of Heroes. An imaginary procession of open-top cars eases by onlookers adulating our national championship. I am in a convertible Mercedes Benz, right arm exhausted from pointing and waving. The shrill blast of a whistle brings me back to reality: our final practice.

"Rotate!" the head coach hollers. Basketball players sprint counterclockwise, sneakers squeaking on the fresh wax. The smell of sweat fills the empty five-thousand seat gymnasium. There is a forty-foot-long banner hanging overhead. It reads: *The NJCAA Welcomes You to New York.*

Our team has reached the pinnacle of success, yet I am mentally absent. I know my days as a Junior College assistant coach are numbered. It has been a grind and I'm ready to retire, done with cramped hours on the road and paisley hotel bedspreads. For the first time in eight seasons, the brotherhood forged over countless hours together is not strong enough to sustain me. Practice continues, but my eyes wander to the past. And the future.

The past: a man isn't a man, I had stated untold times, unless he is respected. An unrespected man is nothing more than a forgotten soul left bloodied on the pathway to the end. Respect is the only measure of success my players need to care about. It is not the boats and cars, houses and jewelry. If a man dies with the respect of those around him, then he dies with everything. That, to me, is the meaning of life: The Secret.

Sitting in the living room of a recruit feels unlike anything else. From the moment pleasantries are over and a seat in the living room taken, there are two minutes to win over a mother or father. In the business this is called *Strike Time*, as in "strike while the iron is hot." I use this time to communicate one critical point: if the player attends my school, there will be more to learn and earn than basketball and a degree. He will leave with The Secret. The parent, without fail, will turn and study their son. I can tell a lot from this moment, about their relationship. If the child locks eyes with the parent, it proves a quality support system with mutual feelings of respect. If the player ignores his parent, it is the opposite almost every time.

By my count, I have coached at least one hundred players over eight seasons. I have worked long hours, sacrificed my free time and opportunities with family to assist these men with The Secret. As a result, or by nothing more than coincidence, the most successful stretch in school history followed: championships, honors, national rankings and records.

The future. What of my own children? I assume that my coaching career affects them: the telephone relationship and vacant seat at the dinner table a constant reminder of my physical absence. And of this, I grow increasingly afraid. There is no respect from children unless it is developed through bedtime tales and basketball in the front yard. I come to the realization that obtaining success as a coach has led to failure of my own advice. I foresee sitting in the living room with one of my children as they meet with a college recruiter, and wonder how, *if,* they will look at me. The unknown is frightening.

Eight seasons has to be enough. Within it are incredible personal tales of student-athletes overcoming obstacles that would make average Americans cast their hands in immediate resignation. Of course, there are failures: well-intentioned men who keep ineptitude a constant companion, bedfellows with the process of bad decision-making. With those men, there is no future and so they live for today. Thankfully, these are but a few. A great many athletes who have passed through our gym door depart on a better road. This achievement though, blended with the abundant victories of my tenure, must not define me. I cannot allow it to comprise more than a few hundred words in my life memoir. If it does, then I have failed. There are greater things.

Practice is over. The head coach stands at center court and we encircle him. I know it will be the last time I huddle with a team. Our hands are interlocked in a wagon-wheel pattern. We count to three and yell "Break" in unison.

The next day we lose by one point and the image of a parade through Main Street falls as flat as a deflated basketball. I had envisioned exiting my coaching career on top, but that cannot be.

Adjacent to our locker room is the hockey arena. I find a quiet place and wedge myself between a Zamboni and a wall of collapsed bleachers. Tears streak my cheeks as I bleat into hands that shake with adrenaline. After a time I find myself silent, with nothing but the cheers from the winning team's locker room to keep me company. I stand, disheveled, and walk away. That's it. I know the players will understand; they need only think back to the first time we met. The Secret will be there.

Months have passed since my decision and not a day goes by with regret. Bedtime tales about lost children and stolen princesses are infinitely more entertaining than watching hours of game film for a player's tendency to give away a crossover dribble.

In hindsight though, I was wrong about one thing. Every Tuesday and Friday afternoon I stand at center court, encircled by my players, our hands interlocked in the middle. The only difference is that my six-foot-four-inch frame towers above the third and fourth grade girls. I take a moment and study my little players, pausing in the eyes of my daughter. Her dynamic coffee-colored gaze meets mine and we share a smile as the team counts to three.

"Break."

Katie Fish *Poetry*

School Halls

Watching them strangely flow
like thin streams of ants,
constantly communicating their next location,
I think—
"How strange I must seem to them
darting and ducking
to avoid crashing their continuous, unified motion,
an individual among their throng.
How strange I must seem
to this crushing flow of ants."

Valentines Day Eve 9:00

I needed eggs for a cake and
drove to a nearby grocery store.
Hours were 8 a.m.-9:30 p.m.
The parking lot was packed
but only a few women were inside.
Crowds of men were in the flower department.
A nervous teenager examined
and held a bouquet of red roses.
He exchanged it for yellow then pink.
An older clerk came to his rescue.
He gave her a smile and correct change
then confidently left with a dozen red roses.
Seasoned lovers grabbed bouquets,
hurried to the checkout, dashed to cars, sped away.
An older gentleman pondered over a plant with a balloon heart
proclaiming "I love you forever." Decision made, he paid the bill
And slowly walked out the door. Mission accomplished.

Susan Perala-Dewey *Poetry*

Sauna Stove Eulogy

Our little cabin sauna stove has gone cold for too long
No one has bothered to stir the embers when ashes started to cool

Now there is little chance to rekindle the flame
Lifeless piles of gray dust cover the rusted floor

Even the walls have collapsed inward from pressure of too much heat at
    once
Parents dying—children leaving home

Once an orange glow peeked through its rectangle window drafts
Inviting simple pleasures of an August summer night

Now it sits steel cold, windows shuttered tight
Blackened door hangs on rusted hinge

It has been too many moons since anyone has bothered to make a proper
    fire
Clear away debris, shovel out ashes and haul them up the hill to where
    raspberries used to grow

To sweep around the hearth, wash away brittle shards of black cinder
Carefully construct a new start with crumpled paper and tinder dry birch

To light a new flame, watch it grow and take off like a flight of starlings
    eager for spring
To tend it, waiting for just the right heat to add more wood

To tenderly wash away the dried salt and grit of mid-life and
Bask in the warm light of glowing embers.

Sheri Smith *Creative Nonfiction*

Social Graces

I was raised, like most children of the fifties with Victorian-minded grandmothers, to never leave the house without clean underwear in the event I ended up in an accident. Despite assurances from medical personnel that they would indeed tend to my injuries no matter the condition of my under-garments, the voice of my grandmother echoes to this day as I prepare to leave the house. Not only do I re-check the state of my underwear, but I always check my make-up, always fluff up my hair, always iron the wrinkles from my clothing, and am always coordinated from head to toe.

Not so my darling husband. Coordinated attire is not his strong suit. In fact, he has at times resembled the Unabomber, happy to live in solitude in a small cabin in the woods wearing the same grubby T-shirt and jeans for weeks on end, until they are so stiff that by all rights they should be used as tinder for a bonfire. As social director and "fashionista" police of our family, it is my responsibility to correct this notion of his that it doesn't matter what he wears. My battle is an epic one.

For example, we attended a company-sponsored golf outing, followed by a picnic. Though it was a casual affair, I stood at my closet for over an hour, contemplating which outfit would allow me to golf comfortably, and match the certain level of chic-sportiness the lovely young wives of my co-workers would surely have found in their own closets. As I am way past young, this clothing selection is always a challenge.

On our drive to the party, I glanced over at my beloved. There were stains on his wrinkled golf shirt the size and shape of the Hawaiian Islands; and a long, white paint dribble resembling the Florida Keys trailed down his khaki shorts. My howl of horror nearly put us in the ditch. "What in god's name are you wearing?" My husband's response was typical, "Just get us back on the road! I look fine!"

My love is not only lacking in social graces, he also has a total disregard for social customs. Not only would he prefer not to attend any and all social functions, but he feels absolutely no guilt in refusing. He's been with his company for sixteen years, and we have yet to attend a Christmas party.

I, on the other hand, feel the need to keep up with any and all social obligations, dragging my husband kicking and screaming to every wedding, baptism, communion, christening, birthday party and holiday get-together within a five state region. The odometer on my aging car reflects the hundreds of miles I've traveled in a single weekend, fulfilling friends and family obligations. My limited closet space is jam-packed with party-specific clothing, worn once and never again seeing the light of day.

Then one day it hit me. My husband sat on the sofa, wearing his most comfortable baggy, slightly stiff denim jeans, looking totally relaxed and without a care in the world.

I, on the other hand, was once again a whirling dervish, getting ready for yet another home party. My bank account was drained, my closet was full, my make-up drawers were spilling over and I was pretty damned cranky. Could I let go of my need to please? I stood with a hanger in hand, draped with a $75 silk blouse that hadn't been worn in so long that it was no longer in style and shoved it to the back of the closet and headed to the bathroom.

Peering deeply at my reflection in the mirror, I wondered what happened to the strong decisive girl I had once been who chose to live her life on her own terms. I surveyed the counters cluttered with knick-knacks, candle holders and useless jumble purchased at previous home decor parties. There was hardly enough space left for me. I made a momentous decision.

I picked up the phone. Although the words stuck in my throat, I was actually able to push out the word, "No," followed by the first statement of decline I'd uttered in fifteen years. *No, I will not be able to attend the plastic storage upgrading event hosted by your second-cousin's niece.*

With a huge sigh of relief, I hung up the phone, feeling the weight of responsibility drop from my shoulders. I donned my gardening jeans, the ones with the ironed crisp pleats, pulled on a sleeveless cotton, polka-dotted shell and layered a color-coordinated striped, open cardigan over that. I sat down on the sofa next to my husband. He put his arm around me. I leaned in close to take a deep cleansing breath of that lived-all-day-in-my-skin aroma he has that makes me feel like I'm truly home.

I've relented on being a fashion freak about my husband's attire. I have learned to say no without feeling guilty. I still attend home parties that truly interest me, dressed in my almost new party-specific clothing. And, as always with a nod to Grandma, I wear clean underwear. Some things will never change.

Frances Ann Crowley *Poetry*

Jack O'Lantern

Now a beautiful teenager
with smooth, orange flesh
he hangs out with friends
at the patch and vineyard.

Soon enough he will be
gap-toothed and gutless
with all his warts showing
no longer handsome
on the outside
but with a certain glow
that comes with age
and a tea light from Walmart.

After some rockin' times
on the porch he will wither
and fall inward—
a gumming grandpa
overripe for compost.

Lucelia Pazar *Fiction*

The Real Events Behind the Expose on the Absent Wunderkind

She was tired of the lights and the questions and the attention. All the attention. She didn't deserve it. She wasn't a genius. She wasn't a master. She was lucky. She was dumb-lucky. Nothing more.

But was it luck? Was it luck when she couldn't open the curtains or walk out of the house without being watched and followed and seen?

She was lucky, or cursed, because the summer she was fourteen, she had gone to Hawaii with her cousins. While they had chased after boys and tried to burn their skin dark brown and golden, she had gone to the reefs. There she had met corals, and a young paleontology student had taken her to the lab and introduced her to the fossil collections, explaining to the best of his knowledge how the path of early evolution flowed. And she had listened and, even through his crush, she could hear sparks of a hidden truth.

The next months of her life were consumed with everything coral, everything astrobiology, everything evolution. But it wasn't just that. She read the Bible and the Book of the Dead. She read primers on Hinduism and Taoism. She knew almost every story ever told about the origin of the world.

And then one day she awoke from a dream, hung over with visions of colonial corals: halysites, favosites . . . And she knew the truth. It exploded out of her fingers as she struggled to write it all down before it disappeared. She didn't eat and hardly drank for the thirty hours it took to write. It was impossible to stop; she couldn't sleep lest she forget it all.

Two years later, she had spoken to NASA, to the Darwin Association, to the Allegiance for Peace. She had spoken before church congregations, stadiums of citizens, and classroom after classroom of disenchanted undergraduates. She had guest-lectured in graduate classes at Oxford, Harvard, MIT and the Sorbonne. There had been talk at more than a few universities of offering her an honorary doctorate. She was famous and everyone loved her, and she was the most unhappy, the most lonely girl in the world. She leaned fondly back in her memory, back to the days of her earliest childhood, when she had danced through the yard, lifting her toes ever higher until finally she was walking through the air, dancing in the sky. She wished she could fly away now, but her feet landed hard on the ground. The higher she jumped, the harder she fell.

When she wrote the first essay about corals, she was in the ninth grade. She wrote what she believed was a convincing argument in favor of further study on corals. Her high school science teacher had looked at it and laughed. "Why do you want to waste valuable minds and valuable resources on such frivolity? Aren't there more worthy causes? Why should your efforts receive more attention than the AIDS vaccine or the cure for cancer?"

She had stared at him wordlessly. Had he even read her paper? If he had, he wouldn't have needed to ask.

That was the last day she went to school. It was October, and she was fourteen. She still had the taste of salt in her mouth, on her skin, left over from summer. She wasn't ready to give everything up. And corals were everything.

So she published the paper, anonymously. Then the journal began forwarding letters. Her heart swelled like flying. And she wrote more, moved beyond the sheer mystery of corals to higher theory. Corals, she posited, contained the most basic roadmap of evolution, and even creation. Her words melted like magic on the keyboard. Again she insisted: corals need more attention and they need it now, while they can be examined alive.

And then the cults sprang up. She had no other way to define them, these groups of people who took her words beyond science and theory and into their spiritual lives. That was the most mystifying part of it all, more than her fame. The public interest was easier to comprehend, because of her youth and gender. Becoming a prophet was never on her list of aspirations, and she resented the take on her words as gospel.

Before her papers reached the heights of underground pop culture, she had carried on healthy correspondences with several interested scientists. One had organized a small team to further her research. Another shared his findings in genetics. Yet another studied the paranormal, and the three of them together had given her hope.

Now they were her only connection to the outside world, to rationality, to sanity.

In addition to her dreams of flight, which may or may not have been memory, she dreamed of Hawaii's shores and the reefs and the lab and her own, dear paleontologist. He had never written and she, fearing his silence indicated resentment because her fame had come first, without education or training, had never tried to contact him. She wished, not for the first time, that she had given him some small reward for his attentions. He had been her last chance, her only chance, at a normal relationship, even though he was older than her by a decade. Everything before her would, by necessity, be based somehow in her public identity. She wanted to be normal. She was, after all, only almost seventeen, and she wanted to be in love. She wished, and then unwished, that she had never met corals, had that dream, or written that paper.

She had become, in essence, a true scientist, despite the romantic ideals of her girlhood. She knew that nothing could be undone.

It was a difficult decision, eased by the flash of shutters each time she approached a front window. She slipped out a back window, where the paparazzi would have difficulty spotting her. She left under cover of shadows. Even the moon hid behind clouds, as if it knew her, and her need. But that was her idealism. The clouds were just vapor; the moon spun mindlessly.

She slipped under the neighbor's fence, as she often had as a child to rescue stray balls. She weaved through yards and alleys until she was in the edges of the city, and then she walked more confidently, the hood of her sweatshirt low over her face.

She had little intention, which was at odds with everything she knew of life these past years. She thought she might visit her uncle, who lived alone in a cabin by the sea. All alone, he had room for one more. All alone, he needed one more. Maybe he would want her, hide her, let her be a child and publish her work in secret.

She thought of her paleontologist. If he were still in Hawaii, if he still desired her, despite her fame, the new shape of her body, he might let her hide in his lab. They could do real research, write papers together.

A crowd made her turn off the sidewalk, into an alley littered with flyers:

Discover your inner polyp!

Connect to the nerve-web of the world!

Discover the self you've always dreamed of!

And here, amidst the evidence of the public's pitiful misunderstanding, and her own lonesome tears, Paige McAllen disappeared.

Birthdays with a First Wife

I still see her lips
Moving in slow motion
Forming promises of love
But I have to believe
She was uncertain of her feelings
Since once a year, for consecutive years
I was given birthday treats
Purchased at the grocery
Or perhaps a high-end gas station
When I flipped the lid open
And stared into the box
The cupcakes were always frosted
Chocolate or vanilla
Candy confetti
Exploded in rainbow colors
Sweet pieces of shrapnel
Scattered across the parchment
But the part that I remember most
Is those scary plastic clown heads
Periscoping through the frosting
While smiling at my discomfort

Nicole Borg *Poetry*

Out of Kansas

I have become a woman
speaking from behind
the green curtain—all invention.

It is her I think of
and her yappy little dog
taking wrong turns,
befriending dummies,
believing in fairy tales
to get back home.

I've forgotten home
except in dreams when
the farmhouse is flying,
the world tears up around me
and the dog won't stop barking.

I remember—
someone died under a great
    weight,
and someone was bitter
and pissed-off and ached inside.

Sometimes,
I think I'm the bitter one
or the crushed one
or the girl who can't get back—
it's hard to tell with dreams,
when each scene is a riddle.

Maybe I am none of these—
the important parts of me
have turned to tin and I've made
an art of forgetting, lying down
with what would destroy me.
I am always too quick to trust
the loudest voice.

Less certain than a road
of brick, I will walk a new path,
tracking that wild animal
who is me. I will feed her
from my hand and all that I've
never said will come out in a roar.

Tarah L. Wolff *Fiction*

Tables

"Why must you drag me to these fricking things?"

"Because it's good for you."

"I'm not going."

"If you go, I'll continue allowing you to believe that you're coming to support me."

So I went. It was a self-help talk. The speaker was always younger, prettier, richer and with a better-looking husband and, most certainly, a better-looking life. This one had written a book called: *Love Your Home*. And its subtitle was: "If it doesn't help you, work for you or if you don't love it—it doesn't belong."

My sister leaned over and sniggered, "I love how she threw that last one in there for those moms who still have thirty-somethings living in their basements who have never helped or worked in their lives." I laughed. At least we could make fun of this one; maybe the afternoon wouldn't be a total loss.

It started the next morning. I can't really explain it except that there was this pan and its handle was loose and I hated it. I made breakfast with the damned thing and I realized, after I emptied the damned thing (of all the scrambled eggs), that it was truly a damned thing. And I wasn't just cranky, it wasn't just me, it was the pan too! I hated it. So I gave my husband the last serving of eggs and promptly chucked it at the garbage can. It hit the back side, body-slammed the can into the wall, almost tipped the whole ship over, then whipped into the bottom with the sound of a shotgun going off in our still and silent kitchen at seven in the morning.

I turned sheepishly to the round eyes of my husband.

He asked, "Whoa! Everything OK?"

I sat down. "I'm sorry!"

He said, "Did it bite you?"

I stared at him, realizing with every part of my being that I could not, even though the pan was still very usable, go get it and continue using it because—"I just hated it."

He rubbed my arm and hand, nodding very enthusiastically. "That's OK, babe! We can get you another one! How old was that? Like a wedding gift?"

I was laughing now. "Yeah! Like a twenty-year-old pan!"

"Well, that's pretty good. It probably only cost us like a dollar a year to use it then! I think it's OK to replace it!" (He is so great. Even now, he knows how frugal I am.)

I still had to justify it even more though. "That damn handle was making my life harder. I had to work for it instead of it helping me make breakfast!"

"Ya know, baby, I don't see why you couldn't just get a whole new set. Ya know, something you pick out, any color you want, whatever you want."

I shook my head. "Oh no no, those other pots and pans are still really great and Grandma got them for us, you know!"

It continued that night when I stopped and stared at my bed. My reading lamp was on and what I mean by "reading lamp," I mean the floor lamp that has been residing by my bed for the last eight years because it didn't work in our office. Its glow highlighted my "bedside table" and when I say that, what I actually mean is a stack of books tall enough to hold a glass of water and an alarm clock without toppling over. It dawned on me that I have never experienced what it's like (since adult-hood) to have a bedside table and it also dawned on me that

that could be a really nice thing. Like a special place to put the books I'm reading and to put a real reading lamp on.

That weekend I dragged my sister to a flea market.

"Why can't you just go to Walmart like everybody else and get a damned table?!"

"I can't do that."

"Why the hell not?"

"Because."

I looked over an old sewing table with interest. She slammed her hand on it. "Waddaya mean?"

I crossed my arms. "I wanna love it! If I'm gonna spend my money and my time getting it and keeping it, I want it just right."

Something flickered in her eyes. "Oh my god! You listened!"

"This is not about any of that self-help bullshit!" I realized at that point that I had just stomped my foot. In the end, I found the right bedside table and it worked out for everybody because my husband happens to have a little woodworking spot in our garage and he never has anything to work on.

It was beautiful (stained and rickety) but solid walnut and, "I got it for a steal! I love it! Would you refinish it for me?"

I don't think I've ever made him so happy.

It happened again the next day in my office when I realized that the horrible (and I do mean horrible) cat-chewed, sun- and water-stained, disgusting blinds that have been in the house since we bought it—were still in the house twenty-two years later.

And I hated them.

My husband stopped asking me, "Why are you getting rid of that?"

I kept getting odd looks from him. The worst was when I actually did decide to give away the whole pots and pans set from our wedding.

"Are you serious? But," he tipped his head at me like a confused puppy, "but, what about your grandma and everything?"

"Listen," I said in my very best I'M OK voice, "they weren't me, they never were. I didn't love them. I loved the thought that went into getting them for me. Grandma will always be with me but I have other things of hers that I love very well. Someone else can use these!"

I caught him later hiding some antiques of his granddad's that he had been keeping (ancient fishing tackle and what-not). After that I simply started sneaking things out and replacing them on my lunch hour.

"Is that a new lamp?" he asked one evening.

"What lamp?"

It started again one evening in the fall. We were sitting on the couch, watching TV and reading. He muted the TV and sighed. Because the silencing of the TV usually means he wants to talk, I stuck my finger in my book and looked his way.

He stared down at the coffee table for a long time. "My granddad built that in an *Ethan Allen* factory in the 1920s—got it for a song because he worked there . . . and it was scratched or some damn thing."

"Yeah. Your dad gave it to you for your twenty-fifth (or something) birthday, didn't he?"

He shrugged. "Eh, well, he thought I needed a coffee table and I don't think he wanted it anymore."

We were quiet for a little while. I sipped my tea, put my book mark in my book and closed it.

He said, "I hate it."

My head snapped up. I stared at him in disbelief. "What?"

He set his mouth. "I hate it."

I thought he loved that thing. I was certain it would be with us the rest of our lives. I hadn't even thought about it.

He got up and proceeded to yell at the coffee table. "You can't put a drink on it! We don't even dare put a damn drink on it when half the damn top of it is covered with fricking coasters. Look!"

I looked. Ten coasters, but all of our glasses were being housed beside us on the end tables of the couch. I never put a thing on that coffee table. If a glass just considered being set down on it, it would simply destroy its "precious" finish.

He continued. "And look at you, baby! You can't be comfortable!"

I was curled up, sitting on my legs, covered in a blanket. I hadn't been caught dead putting my feet on that dainty, fragile, expensive, heavy-as-hell coffee table, since the early years of our relationship. For that matter, I had also never seen him put a drink or a foot on it either.

He said, "I hate it."

I stood up. "Can we take it to the curb?"

His eyes shone with uncertainty. He reached for me and we stared at the coffee table, clutching each other. Two people on the edge of something enormous and frightening.

He said, "I hate it."

I said, "Are you sure?"

He turned me to him and grasped both of my shoulders. "Let's take it to the curb."

It took a month but we found the perfect coffee table. He loves it and I love it and his dad never seemed to notice that the other one was gone.

David Francis *Poetry*

Ricochet

Oh how I like it
when you sit on my desk
leaning toward me.

The readiness in your eye
heats my cheeks.
Your shameless dimple

and improbable high school hair
sculpted wet from the shower
makes white soap smell go reckless.

You've cocked your head,
your eyelids need to close, to rest
from the strain of allure. Yet

you don't pull back,
you're so ready, you barely say,
for anything.

You walk into the room and I
jump, my breath holds, skips
as I see

your pair of faces—
you framed by the window
you framed on the desk. A ricochet

between you and your youth.
Your bloom and your bud,
both you and you and I barely hold.

Jerry Mevissen *Fiction*

Little Women

The daughter's scolding accusations play over and over. *Stupid.* *Disgusting. Stupid.* Funny—the kids were taught to be true to their feelings, but that luxury isn't extended to their parents. Maybe it is stupid. Maybe it looks disgusting. But these emotions are real. They're sincere.

The therapist at the Home says walking is the antidote for whatever ails you—stress, boredom, weight gain. Maybe a walk along the frozen edge of the river will alleviate the stress. Maybe not. It's worth a try.

A feisty wind blows from the east, a harbinger of change in these parts. Change is good. Change is welcome.

It should feel cold, but it doesn't. Nothing feels. Hands are warm in these chopper mitts. Feet, in Sorel boots. Head, in the Elmer Fudd hat that always draws a laugh. Stinging fingers would be welcome, proof there's life in this body.

What time is it? About five. Vera will be rolling her chair to the dining hall at the Home soon. She won't eat. She won't, unless someone's there to coax her. Someone in the family. But no one's there, so she won't eat. It's not too late to drive in, but the doctor said no night driving, no driving when you're stressed, no driving if you're tired. Three reasons not to go.

It's quiet out here. Peaceful. No sound except the crunch of snow underfoot. Owls will hoot soon, Popeye and Olive Owl. Regular residents along the river all winter. Might hear the drumbeat of a pileated woodpecker. Might hear a crow or blue jay squawk and scold, like the kids. Might hear east wind whisper through the white pines, whisper accusations and nod to each other in agreement. *Stupid. Disgusting.*

Vera. My little sparrow. Five-foot nothing. A hundred pounds and shrinking. Not much left to love. So, what now? Is desire supposed to disappear when you're left alone? The kids think so. In her day, Vera was all this man could desire. Tiny, almost miniature, needy in a good way. Irresistible, like a puppy you must hold and squeeze and press against your body and feel the warmth, the softness. Now she lives at the Home.

There are others. There's Colette, my little chickadee, at the super market checkout. Small again. Sensuous and small. Looking like she needs someone to protect her, to shield her. It must have seemed obvious when grocery shopping became a daily routine, always checking out in her lane, making small talk, taking a risk with suggestive banter.

And Penny the hairdresser. Also small and vulnerable. It's more than a lonely man can handle when she wraps her arms around your neck with the cape and presses against you. Then bends you backwards into the sink to massage your scalp. And, oh my God, blows loose hairs off your neck when she's done. Shivers. She deserves a hug, what with raising that toddler alone and trying to make ends meet. She got suspicious when the appointments went from six weeks to five to four. Maybe it wasn't smart to offer her the fifty dollars. But it could have been a loan. It sure wasn't smart to mention it to the kids, which prompted them to call her and ask what was going on. What was going on? Nothing. Or almost nothing. But the hug was worth it. The full body hug around that tiny waist. She didn't pull away, but she didn't hug back either.

The kids say *Stay away. Stay home. Feed your birds. Your nuthatches and purple finches depend on you.* What do they know about a man's needs? *Stay home and play solitaire*, they say. Don't they know solitaire gets boring after a hundred games? Depressing after a thousand? Fatal after a million?

The owl breaks the silence and hoots from the other side of the river. Stop. Listen for Olive Owl's answer. This might be a good place to rest, get off the river, and find a stump to sit on and wait. The trees are tall along the shore here, black silhouettes, undistinguished in their uniformity. The one that bends and wears a foot of snow on its horizontal trunk catches your eye. Isn't that the way it goes? The old timer, the bent guy, gets your attention. May as well keep walking.

There's deer tracks and rabbit tracks and fox tracks, all kinds of tracks. Fun to follow them into the woods and see where they lead. Maybe keep on walking, walk deeper into the woods. Maybe get lost when it gets dark. Maybe have a heart attack and not be found until spring. Maybe not be missed until spring. Maybe that's what they want. *Would serve him right*, they'd say. Better to stay on the river. There's open water ahead where the river shallows.

Hear that rippling sound? That's the rapids, the shallow stretch. It's dark against the white snow. Strange how fast night set in. There's a pale sliver of moon up there. See if there's a spot where the moon reflects on the open water.

Remember last summer when you first saw Penny the hairdresser? Sitting on the beach, nursing her baby, trilling a lullaby? Sand as white as snow, the lake behind her rippling like the river is now, the sun reflecting a trail of gold. Remember the glow of her skin, her pale, angelic skin, the sun creating a halo around her trailing blond hair? Penny, my little canary. *Funny*, you thought. *Vera's from Fargo, but Penny's from heaven.* Don't say that in front of the kids.

The wind's coming up now, shifting to the north. Pines that whispered before shout, a rushing sound like a freight train. It's wind screaming the old refrain, but with gusto. *Stupid. Disgusting.*

A flock of small birds scrambles in loose formation from downriver, finches returning after a day at the feeder. Must be a hundred of them, scrambling, chirping, and chatting. Goldfinches, though not gold now. But when late winter sun hits them, the gold's returning. They can change their color. Maybe there's hope. But they'll change back again next year, so what's the point?

Walking is tiresome. Trudging though snow, breaking trail, heading nowhere. Wishing for an epiphany, a vision, a clue. Nothing. The old birch tree ahead bends down to touch the snow. Must have been uprooted by last summer's wind. Good place to rest.

Something flying up there, big something. Could be an eagle. It is. He's circling. What does he see? Dead meat? Dead man?

Maybe it's a sign. Eagles are medicine birds with magic powers. Good stuff. He's king. He's spirituality and balance and courage in battle. He's a guiding beacon. Might be the reincarnation of a forefather who cares, who understands, who says *Accept yourself the way you are.*

He circles slower, circles lower, lower. He lifts now and heads downriver, heads home, screeching *Follow me, follow me.*

Time Being

Father Earth
revolves in precise
solar propinquity
while Mother Nature
evolves life's
birthing rhythms.

I am their offspring,
brief as a Mayfly,
awakened in warmth
to ride lapping waters,
fly on the wind,
and die in the sand.

I am a poet
in search of words,
measures, and
metaphors,
to resolve the enigma
of my time being.

Eric Chandler *Poetry Honorable Mention*

Bubble

I am not there.
But I am listening.

My little one makes a joke
And your laughter runs down the stairs like a river.
She says it like a question
And you laugh and laugh.
And I would be able to see all your teeth.
My son joins in.
I would make jokes too
If I knew I would be showered with love.

I sit downstairs and lean back in my chair.
I see this bubble of joy in my house.
I am not there.
But I see it floating.
Upstairs.

Laura K. Murray *Fiction*

One Down

Walter opened his eyes to find his cheek stuck to a greasy hamburger wrapper. A teenager with exactly four angry red pimples on his chin was mopping the corner, eyeing him across the restaurant like he was up to no good. Probably thinking he was some homeless bum off the street. Walter couldn't really blame him. Who else falls asleep, dead asleep, inside McDonald's right before dinnertime?

Walter, of course, is homeless, but he certainly isn't a bum. For starters, Walter went to school for a while. He's not a crackhead or a drunk. He doesn't stand by the on-ramp with a piece of cardboard or jump out to clean your windshield at the intersection of Sixth and Washington. Sure, when it's cold like today he pulls on those ratty gloves with the fingers cut out, but lots of people wear those.

Just look at what he's wearing tonight. A dark suit jacket, blue collared shirt, slacks, even a belt. And although you can tell his clothes weren't pressed by any wife of his the night before, you wouldn't notice the fraying hems or the dirty cuffs, or those scuffed shoes either, unless you were right up talking to him, and not many people do that. No, not many people do that.

Plus, when he paid for his double cheeseburger earlier, he made sure to thumb through his cracked leather wallet like he was looking for the right bill before slipping the kid his Y food pass. So you plain wouldn't know Walter doesn't have an address or a doorknob of his own, but you better believe he could just kick himself for falling asleep like that, like an honest-to-goodness bum curled over the tabletop, the scent of those greasy fries warming up his nostrils.

Everybody at Mickey D's—that's Walter's nickname for the golden arches—watches him come in each day and sit in the corner booth with his coffee. They know he'll grab exactly five ketchup packets. Five.

They know this because Walter takes the packets one at a time, plucking them each precisely out of the container next to the straws. Sometimes just to make things interesting he'll take one, two, three, four. Then he'll wait a beat, acting like he doesn't notice everybody in the place watching him sideways. He'll maybe even turn like he's ready to go sit down, and then *snatch!* He'll grab number five and, man alive, if you can't hear the sigh of relief clear across the parking lot to the SuperAmerica next door.

Walter tucks the packets in the pocket of his beat-up briefcase. The pocket is bulging with what do you think? Ketchup packets. Always ripping open too, so that if you were to open the zipper, and you probably wouldn't do it, you'd see the inside coated with dried tomato paste and slippery plastic.

Now that Walter's awake, he turns back to the folded newspaper laying under his arm and picks up his pencil. Its eraser is worn clean off because Walter isn't what you'd call talented at crosswords, truth be told. It's not his fault he's a numbers man! Floor tiles, concrete blocks, freckles, coat buttons, ketchup packets, he can have them counted up in a jiffy by hardly glancing at them.

Jimmy was the ace at crosswords. Walter could sit there for hours, scribbling in letters and erasing them out again until his brain hurt. But Jimmy—you'd spend twenty minutes trying to come up with the answer to five across, four letters, and seconds after looking at the clue he'd say something like, "Leda," like he did once, and it'd fit just perfect. And then you'd ask him about it and he'd tell you Leda was this Greek lady who got raped by a swan who—get this—turned out to be the Zeus, the head honcho himself, married to boot.

You had heard of Zeus but never knew he was such a creep. And all you can do is sit there with your head spinning and say, "No kidding" and wonder where he learned all that.

Jimmy was homeless too. He came into Mickey D's one day, and Walter could tell right off the bat he was new to this not-knowing-where-you-were-going-to-sleep business. Walter offered him a seat, and Jimmy offered him half his Egg McMuffin as he worked on Thursday's crossword. It wasn't easy having two of you to think about, but Walter didn't mind. Especially when folks started locking the church doors at night so you couldn't have a quick and holy liedown in the back pew, and instead you had to crowd under a bridge or curl up next to the buffalo statue by the library. It was kind of cozy knowing someone else was there too, keeping an eye out. It was nice to have someone to talk to, or even someone not to talk to.

And Walter tried talking to people, he really did. The problem was he got a little nervous about it.

Once, the man in the next booth with seventeen gray hairs growing out of his ear asked to borrow the sports section and, before Walter could stop himself, he was going on about crosswords and Jimmy and how good he was at them and asked if he had ever heard of this knock-out woman named Leda, and the man with the seventeen gray hairs looked at him like he was a loony and you can bet he left that sports section right where it was.

Yessir, Walter sure missed having someone to talk to. The way things were now he'd be walking down the sidewalk or looking over the paper and say something to nobody. Sometimes he'd pretend it was Jimmy.

"Man alive, is it cold out here," he'd say, or, "Oh, would you look, Bloomingdale's is having a sale. Just in time for our winter wardrobe, too." He and Jimmy were always joking like that.

You be sure, Walter talked very quiet-like when he did this so nobody would think he was a loony, which was worse than being a bum, if you didn't know. You have to be careful about that sort of thing. People watch a guy real close if they think he's got a screw loose.

Some days Walter'd go morning to night without talking one peep. His throat got so hoarse he just had to say something, even if it was to his reflection in the restroom mirror or a shadow under a streetlight. Car horns, grease fryers, stray dogs—so much noise but none of it talked back.

Jimmy would disappear sometimes and show up again with red-rimmed eyes and shaky hands. He couldn't concentrate on the crosswords when he was like that. Walter told him he had to stop with that stuff—didn't Jimmy know it was the surest sign you were a bum? And those two, they certainly weren't bums.

One morning Walter had woken up on his cot in St. Anne's basement and Jimmy wasn't anywhere. The wrinkled old guy supervising the breakfast line said Jimmy had lit out in the middle of the night. He never showed up at Mickey D's, although Walter stayed in the corner booth all day.

That was six years ago, and Walter hadn't finished a crossword yet.

Walter wasn't worried, though. See, what Walter figured happened was Jimmy hopped a train to the desert. Jimmy was always talking about the desert. They'd planned to hitch a ride out west soon, out where you could just crawl into the hot sand and bake right into the earth. Where you could sleep under the sky all year long and listen to the emptiness and never run out of stars to count. It'd be hot as the devil's armpit, but nobody would mistake a guy for a bum out there.

Jimmy had wanted to check out the desert and make sure it was as good as he had been saying, Walter knew. That was the thing about Jimmy, he always had to be right. He'd probably come strolling through the door to Mickey D's any day, order his Egg McMuffin with his five packets of ketchup, plop down, and stab at the paper.

"Eleven down, 'Patton.' That's O-N."

The restaurant was crowding up fast as folks lined up for dinner. Walter cleared his throat a few times and carefully slid the unfinished crossword into his briefcase. He smoothed his suit jacket and pulled on his coat, fastening its three buttons and two safety pins. Outside, he looked up at the darkening sky. If his nose was right, and it usually was, snow was coming. He figured he had about an hour until dark.

Sonja Kosler *Poetry*

Phases

maple leaves shiver
as mice skitter to pantries
harvest machines rest
   half-moon wanes toward her darkness
   where poet words pause then die

Kelly Nelson *Poetry*

Fire Science

Inspect this house—
its one door, its meager windows.
Cross check the chance of rain with the west
prairie wind. Time of day: 2 a.m. The year: 1940.

This is the farmhouse where my mother was born.
In the kitchen, her drunk father fumbles to light a cigarette.

Measure the water's speed
from the ground, the slim width
of the table legs. Synchronize the hands
of the clock with the spark on the rag rug.

Five people in the next room sleeping.
Now, tell me why only two made it out alive.

Small Griefs

I should have done as you, Mary Oliver,
the little coin of flesh, so strange
and pink, so alien. Not a child yet.
No, not a child.

I took it with me
in the smallest container
I could find, cradling it awkwardly
in the waiting room, so the midwife
could tell me what I
already knew.

I should have brought it home—
I should have found a tree
with somber purple leaves.
I should have knelt in the sun-warmed earth
and dug a hole just large enough
for small griefs.

Chet Corey *Poetry*

Gone

I have let a poem sit to cool
like those old women in small towns
along railroad tracks
during the Depression and Dust Bowl
would let hot apple pie cool
on an open kitchen windowsill
only to have some hobo
come along drawn by the aroma of it.
And like those homemaker women
in their good baking hearts
I've hoped it was shared with others.

Sharon Tauber *Creative Nonfiction*

The Seasoned Palate

I was in South America visiting my daughter who had just spent six months studying abroad in Chile. Our wanderings took us to San Pedro Market in Cusco, Peru. Once beyond the booths of tourist trinkets in this cavernous building we encountered row upon row of brightly colored fruits and vegetables, flowers, herbs and spices, grains, giant wheels of golden bread, cheese, brown eggs . . .

A menagerie of well-ripened fruit inside glass enclosures shouldered numerous juice bars, and I longed to savor the sweetness they offered. Steaming cauldrons surrounded by lunch counters dispensed bowls of dense soup that floated whole chicken legs. I wanted to taste the rich flavors of the soup, but all I could think about were the warnings in the travel guides to not drink the water and to be careful about what you eat. The warnings must be effective because it appeared that the only people enjoying this feast were Peruvian.

We passed by the food booths and found ourselves in a long isle flanked by a Peruvian meat market. I stopped to look at a beef tongue. "Boy, they really got the whole root on those; they're huge," I said as my daughter hurried on. Lagging behind, I let my mind slip along the smooth maroon surface of the liver before me, back to the farm in west-central Minnesota where I grew up.

Mom doused pieces of liver and heart in flour and fried them in lard. I preferred the sweet chewiness of the heart over the mealy liver. The tongue was boiled, then marinated in vinegar and, when cold, sliced to make a tender, dense sandwich meat.

I caught up with my daughter by a display of hooves, whole heads and a row of snouts. "I have to get out of here," she said, looking a bit pale. I smiled after her as she headed away down the aisle looking neither right nor left. Turning back to the counter I couldn't decide if the heads and snouts were from cows, horses, or mules.

All I know about are pigs' heads. Every fall two men from the neighborhood brought out a rusty half barrel that rested on wooden stands. Our choicest pig was bled out, rolled whole in boiling water in the barrel, shaved smooth, hung by its back hooves and severed. For the next week our kitchen became a processing plant. Mom boiled the pig's head with the organs, meat scraps, spices, and onions. The cooked meat was ground into what we called liver sausage. We piled it hot on homemade bread and topped it with ketchup or sliced radish. The pig's ears, along with the hooves and other cartilaginous parts, went into pickled-pigs'-feet. Each of us kids took our turn cranking the fat through the cast iron grinder clamped to the edge of the kitchen table. Mom cooked down the fat into lard that was used for frying and for baking pie crust, bread and cookies. The leavings from making lard, called cracklings, were the bits of deep-fried gristle and meat that settled to the bottom of the pot. Cracklings were crunchy and tasty fresh, as they drained on brown paper, or baked into oatmeal cookies as a substitute for raisins or chocolate chips.

My daughter had disappeared. I moved past the piles of intestines and what appeared to be esophagus, past slabs of red meat to the poultry. Pimply-skinned chickens lay in rows on the counter, their feet poking out at me. Next to whole chickens was a pile of chicken feet.

We were a large family. We fought over the two chicken feet that come with one chicken. It would have been a culinary dream to have a whole pile of chicken feet. After the feet, my favorite part of a chicken was the tail, fried crisp. Too often I'd grab for the back, salivating over the prospect of the tail, only to find Mom had devoured the tail while pulling the pieces from the frying pan. The gizzard or heart could have soothed my disappointment but, by the time I noticed the missing tail the gizzard and heart had been snatched from the platter.

I didn't see in San Pedro Market many of the things that were staples in our diets: venison, wild duck and pheasant, sunfish, crappie, northern, squirrel, rabbit, pigeon, dandelion greens, wild grapes, chokecherries and gooseberries . . .

It wasn't until I was older that I realized most Americans have not grown up with the opportunity to season their palates the way I did. What I consider to have been a privilege was, in reality, a necessity. Just like Peruvians of today, we could not afford to let anything go to waste.

I found my daughter by a stall where stiff canvas sacks were rolled back to display an abundance of benign dried beans, corn, lentils and legumes. We headed back to the main plaza, passing a street vendor with a display of roasted guinea pig splayed flat with head and feet intact. That I could never eat.

On the way back to our three-star hotel we stopped at a restaurant that was packed with American and European tourists. The wait staff was almost as tall and as pale-skinned as us. While I ate the American-looking sandwich I had ordered, I regretted not having tried the soup at San Pedro Market. I would probably make it home without intestinal issues but, like my daughter, who would never experience the reality of growing up on a farm during lean times, I would be going home without having experienced the true Peru. She was staying in Peru for another four months. She might develop a taste for guinea pig.

Linda M. Johnson *Poetry*

Just Once

I'd like to tip my head back
when there's a second full moon in a month
I'll bare my teeth and summon disappointment
from the depths of my being
forcing it to rise until it gains velocity
speeds up, up through my throat
into my mouth where it erupts in a howl
and I won't stop
until one by one animals pause to listen
and even wolves themselves will
venerate the way vibrato throbs in my voice
and fur on their necks will
arise to salute me—
a mere, howling human
and I'll yowl about yesterday's regrets and
today's mediocrity and I'll pour out every sin
and frustration to the man in the moon
my false Catholic confession
I can't see the moonman
any more than I can see the priest
and finally, when I spew all that I can
and my system purges itself of discontent
I'll draw in an endless star-studded breath
until the space I hollow inside myself glows
just once

Sangita Kalarickal *Fiction*

Intervention

"Are you absolutely sure?"

The deep voice reverberated in Shanta's brain and jolted her out of her almost hypnotic state. Eyes round and heart thumping madly, she looked at the man in awe. Her idea of generic tantrics and godmen did not do this man's presence justice. She had imagined lines on his forehead drawn with grey ash and red vermillion, golden sandalwood paste art on his bare chest. But nothing of the sort. This man did not need such embellishment to capture her mind and soul. Only an iridescent pearl set in gold adorned a finger, trying in vain to compete with the light that shone from his dark brown eyes. Yet, with his white shirt, dark khakis and leather sandals, the simple-looking man might as well have been the guy in the next cubicle hammering away at his computer.

She was drawn to this mystic as though his power lassoed her and pulled her all the way several hundred miles from the large city she called home to the little village in the tropics where he lived and worked.

This man was known to offer solutions, and hers was merely one act away.

She was desperate.

Last year a mislaid phone revealed the signs of a failing marriage to an oblivious Shanta.

The frequency of Jay's business trips had increased but, caught up with her successful career and kids, she was unconcerned. Her ten year investment in the marriage felt solid and secure. Ten years of her youth, ten years of her loyalty. Ten years of her slowly falling in love with the man picked for her by her family. Never mind that she didn't have a decent conversation with Jay before their engagement. Never mind that their marriage was a result of persistent matchmaking. Time spent in setting up home worked its magic in transforming a ritualistic relationship into one that bound her heart to her husband. Her house transformed into a home. Their extended families doted on her two daughters, often competing for a chance to babysit. Shanta was happy.

But the illusion of that perfect life vanished the day she absent-mindedly picked up Jay's phone and spotted an incoming text.

"Lu 2."

Her heart first skipped a beat and then started pounding in her ears. Who in the world would write "love you too" to *her* husband?

A few months, and she unraveled the mystery spiraling into a nightmare of deceits and lies, of disappointments and disillusions.

Pooja Patwardhan was his colleague. Men tripped over themselves to be around the pretty woman, almost drooling every time she laughed, throwing her head back, her hair flying about.

Shanta knew she could offer no competition to this alluring twenty-something. When confronted, Jay denied everything. The text messages, the faint perfume that refused to leave his shirts.

"How can you not trust me?"

"You're hallucinating. There's nothing, nothing going on."

"She's just a friend. A *friend!*"

"You are becoming a clinging paranoid witch!"

When the bickering started giving her daughters nightmares, she stopped asking him. Shanta stewed slowly, betrayal hacking away at her, draining her tears until there were none left.

He might walk out on her, her daughters. Her love for him meant nothing, this she knew now. Every time the thought of being left alone with the kids struck her, her stomach fired a volley of bile up her throat. Fear of being shunned by her family. And the shame!

Her nights were marked by wide open eyes, unshed tears burning her lids. Her grief at Jay's betrayal gave a slow boil into rage against Pooja.

Then she heard of the mystic.

The tantric, who had mastered ancient spells. Honed over two thousand years and several generations, the skill was inherited. His witchcraft was widely known. Also well-known was his reluctance at performing black magic for pay. It had taken her two days to convince Shashibhushan Paniker to listen to her story. Two days of weeping. For two days she arrived early at his doorstep and sat on a dusty mat on the front porch. He refused to talk to her but when he returned from his visit to the village, or the temple, she was still waiting. Her tears and persistence implored him to finally listen to her "What will my daughters do?" and "We will be left alone!" and begged him to avenge her betrayal, to find her peace, to make Pooja leave Jay. Jay may never walk out of the relationship on his own, so maybe the girl could find another man, maybe an unmarried one.

Shanta needed that to happen.

The village scorched in the sultry heat of summer, a heat that could lull senses into inactivity. Dense canopy of green created by coconut palms and mango trees offered no respite. Tiny sweat beads formed on Shanta's forehead and she frowned at the slow, squeaking ceiling fan which did nothing more than add a rhythmic tune to an otherwise quiet afternoon. Used to air-conditioned rooms, Shanta squirmed in discomfort. Slender wisps of smoke swirled from sandalwood incense sticks and dissolved into the humid heat, saturating the room with its sweet heady fragrance. Shanta clenched her fists until her knuckles shone white as she sucked in the hot air infused with incense, filling her lungs until it hurt.

"Are you absolutely sure?" he repeated, slight impatience creeping into his voice.

She breathed out a puff of air in a deep sigh. Her dry tears stung her eyes. Of course she was sure.

"Yes." Her voice trembled. "I want her out of his life."

"You know there is no turning back," he warned. His deep-set eyes bored directly into her soul. A chill ran down her body, attacking one bone at a time. "Once I begin the rituals," he leaned forward, "events will be set in motion that cannot be stopped. You want the woman out of his life. There are several ways of doing that. I cannot control which one."

"Yes," Shanta whimpered. Fear had transformed her life into a putrid blend of unwanted emotions. She was scared of what she was going to do.

Scared of this gentle yet powerful man before her. Scared of the vast lonely life if she did not intervene.

Yet this seemed to be the most effective solution.

"You know the cost of the rituals."

Shanta nodded.

"You may leave the money on the table there," he continued. "Walk out directly, no need to look back. I will take care of the rituals. You go home."

Shanta's face wrinkled in uncertainty. She paused as his instructions sank in, and then stood, her legs wobbly from sitting cross-legged on the hard floor. She fumbled in her purse for the money and staggered towards the door. She left the envelope on the small wooden table and walked out the door, into the palm-riddled courtyard. She did not look back.

Sunlight peeped out through the dense foliage cover. Her heart suddenly felt light. A slight spring crept into her steps. Jay was away on a trip again, but this time when he returned it would be different. The crisis would soon be behind her.

Shanta looked forward to the evening. Jay would soon return from his latest business trip. She packed the kids off to their aunt's home to spend the night with their cousins and lovingly prepared dinner. Aroma of spices from his favorite mutton curry lingered in the air.

This evening would be different, unforgettable she promised. The visit to Shashibhushan Paniker filled her with a confidence she had long forgotten. She had dressed carefully in Jay's favorite blue and even applied makeup.

This will be a night he'd remember. She caught a glimpse of her reflection in the mirror and Shanta's face broke into a smile. *This is it.*

The phone pealed. She frowned before she picked it up. *No. No distractions tonight. I'll turn it off after he arrives.*

"Mrs. Raghavan?" a male voice asked.

"Ye . . . s, who's calling?"

"I'm calling from the police station, madam. I'm sorry. Your husband was in a car accident. He's no more." His voice softened.

Shanta's mouth went dry. Her voice refused to slide up to her tongue. A cold draft of air draped in sandalwood incense swirled around her. Her grip on the phone tightened.

"But . . . " her cracked voice stuttered. "He was to *fly* back."

"Well," the policeman's voice lowered. "Madam, his colleague Miss Patwardhan was driving him back. She drove into an oncoming truck. The way she suddenly swerved, witnesses thought she was drunk. But no . . . it looks like an unfortunate accident." Her grip slackened and her trembling fingers released the phone. She watched for a moment through a surreal haze, as the phone clattered on the floor.

The mystic's voice drifted through the alleyways of her foggy mind.

Are you absolutely sure?

Susan Niemela Vollmer *Poetry*

Book

I finished the last chapter of this book
and now I need to read back to find out
why the woman married that man
although I know, of course,
that it is in some way because of the child

I had skimmed the first chapters
but they were so dark, almost macabre
that I skipped ahead to the end
hoping that knowing the conclusion
would make the beginning easier to bear

Beth Diane Bradley *Creative Nonfiction*

Living Alone . . . Selfish is the New Sexy

Who knew? Living alone is now trendy and hip. I've recently seen two stories about this in the media. About four years ago I became a divorced empty nester, and found myself living alone for the first time in over twenty years. It didn't take long for me to become—well, there is no other word for it—*eccentric*. They didn't list that as one of the very hip qualities of those who live alone by choice.

I don't mind being eccentric, as I am a writer and writers are supposed to be weird. But there is that point where weird starts to turn into crazy. For example, I've brought my childhood imaginary friend back to life, but with a grown-up attitude. She likes to hear about my latest culinary adventures, and puts up with my ranting at political ads on TV. When I was a kid, she merely told me not to eat Brussels sprouts.

It doesn't hurt to talk to her when I'm alone in my apartment, but sometimes we continue to chat in my car, office, or the grocery store—until I notice people are staring. Busted! It's time to pretend I'm a secret agent talking into a cleverly concealed recording device.

People who live alone also like eating serial for supper—that's right, I mean serial, not cereal (although that *also* works). Meaning, if you cook, you get to eat the same thing every day for a week. This is especially effective in causing mutations, due to the lack of nutritional variety. Just say yes to individuality!

Another opportunity afforded only to those of us who are "single by choice" is unusual menus. I hate to throw out food, so I often end up with an odd collection of leftovers, and pretend it's normal to eat them together. Close your eyes and imagine a quarter cup of chili, a half a grapefruit and some day-old popcorn. My imaginary friend still thinks this combination is better than Brussels sprouts.

A classic fear expressed by many who live alone is dying and not being found for days. This is another job for your imaginary friend. Teach her to dial 911 on her imaginary cell phone and everything will be OK.

According to the news stories, the benefits of living alone include hogging the remote, eating crackers in bed, using all the hot water . . . in other words, regressing to toddler-hood. Hey, selfish is the new sexy. It gives you that "I don't give a damn" attitude that drives the opposite sex wild. "Oh, baby, you know what I like." But then if that really worked, living alone would no longer be trendy and hip.

I do recommend having a pet to keep you company. I have two dogs, and they are much more agreeable than a lot of human companions. The difference between living with just pets, and living with pets and people—is how you relate to them. My dogs have replaced my two grown sons. They actually share the bedroom my youngest son used to occupy. But the difference is they have less stuff. And you can't yell at them for not picking it up, because they don't have thumbs.

I talk to my dogs even more than I talk to "you know who." They obviously don't talk back, but they do understand. My new thing is trying not to eat so fast, so I attempted to make conversation with my dogs while eating lunch this noon. I took a bite, put the fork down, and then asked them a question. OK, I don't need your opinion on this one . . . weird just turned into crazy. Tomorrow, I'm getting a parrot!

Can I Please Take it Back?

you've never looked more beautiful
than in the hour after I dumped you

with affection
I apologize

someday your son or daughter
will find a picture of me
and they will know
that for a time
I loved you

Georgia A. Greeley *Creative Nonfiction*

The Dance

It startled him as I drove up in the truck. Breezes rattled the leaves. He was splitting wood, stroke by stroke, thinning logs to wood-stove size. He'd been alone in our isolated shack in the woods for a week. He was in coveralls; I was still in uniform. The sun was slanting towards evening, gilding every leaf and blade of grass it touched. I slipped off the truck seat and my feet touched the ground. He looked up at me with such joy on his sweaty, unshaven face, as if he were a sunflower raising its petals to the awakening sun. He lodged his axe into a chunk of wood with a hearty thwack. I walked towards him and he opened his arms. I walked in. He whooped and whipped me around the wood pile in a wild dance of high-stepping feet and laughter, the most primitive music. We stopped and held each other so tight I stopped, fearing I'd topple over from the uncontrolled trembling in my muscles. Unexpected as a rainbow without rain, this silly, wonderful dance, blessed by the setting sun.

Sea and Sand

Beach sand clings to wet feet like henna-drawn tattoos,
waves wash the shore like pale tumbled jade.

The near white sands speak of ocean days, but
there is no salty tang here on Superior's freshwater shore.

These Apostle Islands scatter out like dice tossed
by a deft hand. Shore birds strut past,

balance on driftwood, and scavenge for food.
Today's waves kick up an easy wind that tickles the spiky

clumps of beach grass into gentle backbends.
Given the slightest bit of attention they graciously bow.

Miles away, in the grasslands of Kansas, Amareitha will wear
her hand-sewn sari; women will paint her hands with henna.

They'll decorate her feet with intricate reddish-brown curls
in the tradition of her Sri Lankan family, and heads

will bow as the new couple emerges.
All attention will be theirs.

Sue Reed Crouse *Poetry*

Code Breaking

There must be a message
from you down here,

hidden in one of the damp boxes
stored in your basement bedroom—

I'm fine
        or   *send help.*

I think I hear a conversation of ghosts.

A code in the crumbs,
rattling like a rain stick
inside your thrift-store toaster,

a cipher coating the butter knife,
disguised in the smear
of your last meal,

a halo in the coffee ring,
clinging to the inside
of the seagull mug,

which I bring to my ear like a secret phone.

Sharon K. Donohue *Fiction*

Eye of the Beholder

Darkness and mist lay like a shroud over Pacific Heights, the street lamps casting a morbid glow. An old woman bent with age slowly makes her way up the street clutching her cloak tightly around her, the raised hood exposing only a few wisps of white hair. One trembling, gloved hand protrudes from a cloak vent holding fast to a plain brown cane. She does not hurry; her galoshes make a slight shuffling sound as she walks.

She appears to be quite unaware of the dangers of the night around her but, truth be known, she is tense with apprehension. There has been talk and newspaper accounts of women being accosted and left in a bad way for the police to find later. The women were mostly uninjured; however, the humiliation and emotional damage could last a lifetime. It has been assumed to be the work of some young toughs who think they can get away with anything and often do.

"Three more blocks," she whispers. Vision is poor in the gloom and mist, but she can just faintly hear laughing on the corner up ahead. She really wants to turn and go back the way she came, but it had been such a long hard walk already. "Have to just keep going," she mutters to herself.

As she approaches the corner, the laughter stops, and she can feel the eyes upon her. Two men, their faces muffled by the foggy mist; then a voice cracks out, "Hey, what do we have here; perchance a lovely morsel?" As she draws closer, his tone changes to disappointment. Another voice chimes in, "Any port in a storm, eh Mick?"

"Naw, Jacko, it's just an old lady."

"No, I think I like old ladies," quips Jacko. "Maybe she has a purse."

"You're not that hard up for cash, bucko," admonished Mick.

The old woman, cringing slightly, shuffles by, almost closing her eyes with fright, forcing herself to keep moving, her trembling cane tapping along the sidewalk.

"Go on, Granny, have a nice night." That one was Mick.

"You also," her thin, quavering voice comes back. Finally at the curb stepping down. *Be careful*, she thinks, *don't trip*. Starting across the street, the sound of a car overtakes the heavy silence. *I won't make it*, she thinks and takes a step back against the curb. She can still feel eyes watching her as she stands there bent over her cane, waiting. The car speeds past and squeals around the corner, drawing the eyes of the two men. She tries to hurry a little to get across the street. Stepping up on the far curb, she breathes a shaky sigh of relief; only two more blocks now. She moves closer to the street edge of the sidewalk to get more distance from the darkened doorways. Taking a deep breath and continuing to the next corner, aware of the deepening pain in her back and trying not to hurry too much, just keeping a steady pace; the cane helps with that. At the end of that block, a right turn and halfway down the hill and home. "Oh my God," she sighs. "I need to stretch. 1529, I'm home!" She climbs the steps carefully, not too fast, using the cane. She unlocks the door, steps shakily through and closes the door tight. Safe on home base.

"Oh! Hello, Mother. You're up late."

"Not as late as you, dear heart. I've been too worried about you to sleep. I'm so relieved you're home."

"Me too, Mama," replies the old woman, shrugging off her heavy cloak, and stretching as tall as her five-foot-six-inch frame will allow, carefully working out the painful kinks from being hunched over for so many blocks. After hanging up the cloak, tucking the white wig into the hood, she lets her long, auburn hair unwrap and fall down around her shoulders and down her back. Kicking off the galoshes, she turns to her mother. "Come on, Mama. Let's go put the kettle on for tea, and I'll tell you all about my part in the new play."

Kathryn Knudson *Poetry Editor's Choice*

South of the K-Mart on Lake

Here two blocks south of the K-Mart
on Lake Street you don't live or rent

and you almost never buy. You stay.
Anything else sounds too permanent.

An uncle's drug habit is talked about
in sighs but what's being said is

understood. A baby's father drifts out
and back in again like smoke you can't

keep from inhaling. You're told it is what
it is; what you think doesn't matter. And

eventually you could start seeing it
the way most other folks do, like

living room furniture that never looks
quite right. You can keep rearranging

the furniture, even replace it all, but
why bother. It's the room too.

Marsh Muirhead *Poetry*

My Madness

In the end it will be the little stickers
that push me over the line—
the smiley faces with bar codes
quantifying the peaches and apples,
the plums and avocados in my cart—
stickers, the store manager informs me,
which are required for quality control
and freshness, inventory management.
And not only that, he says,
the average cashier—you know
a young person—
wouldn't know a pear from a kumquat
if they bit one.
And so, on the day
that the awful and surprising news
reaches you, know that you will find
apple skin and bits of paper
under my fingernails,
nectarine juice and traces of ink
on my lips, fresh fruit in my kitchen
which I hope you will take home
and share with our friends.

Dennis Herschbach *Fiction*

Girl With the Red Bike

Pastor John rang the doorbell, and from inside came a high-pitched, reedy voice. "Come in," it invited.

He let himself in and was greeted by the smell of mothballs and the sight of Evelyn hunched over her dining room table.

"Good morning, Pastor," she called out before he could say a word. "Isn't it a beautiful day?" She dragged out the word beautiful so it was almost the width of a page.

"Come look out the window at the lake. It's so blue today and the whitecaps are so white. I saw an eagle fly by only two minutes before you drove down the driveway. It was lovely, just lovely."

Pastor John sat down beside her and looked out the window. Evie, as everyone called her, had been tall once, well over six feet, but now she was bent almost double, hardly able to stand.

"I baked your favorite, chocolate chip cookies, today. And I've already poured your coffee." She pushed the plate of cookies and cup and saucer at him.

"Do you like fruitcake?" she asked, and before Pastor John could answer, she asked another question. "Did I ever tell you about the first time I made fruitcake?" Again, he didn't have time to answer.

"Well, I was a young housewife and didn't know much about baking, so I followed a recipe. It said to soak the raisins in an expensive-sounding liqueur, but we only had booze so I used that instead.

"I figured if soaking the raisins was good, soaking all the fruit would be even better. So I dumped the whole mess in a bowl and added a cup or two of booze."

Once Evie began a story, there was no stopping her. All one could do was sit back and enjoy, which wasn't difficult.

"The recipe said to let the raisins soak for two hours. I got busy on something else and forgot the fruit in the refrigerator. The next morning, when I was making breakfast, I was reminded by the bowl of booze-soaked fruit in the refrig that I was going to make fruitcake. By that time, wouldn't you know, all the booze had been soaked up by the fruit so I added a little more.

"I mixed up the batter and stirred in the fruit, poured it into three fruitcake pans, and placed them in the oven. Then I went into the living room to read a magazine while they baked.

"I had only been sitting for about ten minutes when I heard a large explosion in the kitchen, and I rushed to see what had happened. The door to the oven had blown open and all the waxed paper under the fruitcakes was on fire. Almost scared the life out of me. Well, I put the fire out, and the fruitcake seemed OK." There was a perfectly timed pause.

"And you know, the oven blew open three more times before the fruitcake was done baking."

Pastor John could hardly wait to get home to sample Evie's Christmas fruitcake.

His next visit was three weeks later and began much the same way. He thanked her for the delicious fruitcake, hoping there would be another offering. Evidently, Evie had eaten the rest.

"Pastor, did I ever tell you about the time Judy and I went shopping in Chicago?" He started to say "No," but before he could open his mouth, Evie cut him off.

"Well, Judy and I got on the train in Duluth and headed for Chicago. We wanted to get away from our husbands and planned to shop for the weekend. Don't you think Judy is a sweet person? Did you know she boxed with her brothers when she was young? Usually beat them up, too.

"Well anyway, we were having so much fun in Chicago that we each decided to buy a wig. There was a shop near our hotel.

"Judy and I waltzed right in, but all they had were black wigs. Then we realized that they catered to African-Americans. Anyway, we each bought a huge, frizzy Afro wig . . . wore them all weekend. People looked at us kind of strange though."

Judy and Evie were both Norwegian, Evie over six feet tall and Judy, barely five. That image stayed with Pastor John for a long time after he left her home.

One day in summer, during his regular visit, Evie asked if she had ever told him about the girl on the red bike. He didn't have time to shake his head.

"When my husband was alive he loved to fish. I would go with him, sit on shore and read in the shade while he was out in his boat. His favorite place to fish was up the shore near a small village, Hovland. Do you know where that is?

"Well, this one day I was reading my book, and a little girl kept riding her red bicycle in a circle around and around me. Finally, she stopped and stared. I said, 'My that's a nice bicycle you have, sweetie.'

"She looked at me and said, 'Yeah, but it was all shot to hell, before my dad fixed it.'

"We visited all afternoon. I even shared my lunch with her, but my Lord, you couldn't repeat the words that came out of the little tyke's mouth.

"Later in the afternoon her father came to retrieve her.

"'I hope Cindy Lou didn't bother you too much. I know, her mother was a big fan of Dr. Seuss. Anyway, Cindy's mother died three years ago, and since then it's just been the two of us.

"'I'm a logger, and the only people she sees are my logging buddies. I'm afraid she's picked up some pretty crude words.'

"Before they left for home," Evie continued, "I said I'd be willing to babysit Cindy if he ever went to Duluth to get away. Wouldn't you know, a week later he did just that, left her with me for the whole weekend.

"Her visits became a regular thing. We would have tea parties, go shopping, do things little girls do. I tried to teach her to be a lady.

"I haven't seen Cindy for years, but she always sends me a birthday card. Would you like to see what she sent this year?" Evie held it up so he could see.

Pastor John would make his regular rounds of home visits about every three weeks and, every time he stopped, Evie had a plate of fresh-baked chocolate chip cookies for him.

"Have another cookie, Pastor. You've only had three. Are they burned on the bottom?" She pushed the plate toward him, and he couldn't help but notice how bent and weak her hands were becoming.

The next time Pastor John visited Evie, she was in the hospital.

"Pastor, will you look in that corner?" She pointed to an upper corner of the room. "Tell me if there is a hole there, because last night a continual stream of bugs were moving up and down the wall over there."

Pastor John looked. "No, there is no hole. Perhaps your medication was making you see things."

"Oh darn," she said. "They were so cute I wanted them to be real." That was the last time he visited Evie.

Pastor John officiated at her funeral. It was at times a sad affair and at times jubilant as story after story was told of her escapades. He was about to close that portion of the service when a stately lady walked down the church aisle and took the microphone. In a teary voice she said, "I don't know where I would be if I hadn't met Evie. She saved me when I was a little girl. I loved her like she was my mother."

As she handed the microphone back, Pastor John looked her in the eye and said. "I'll bet you had a red bicycle when you were a little girl."

She smiled through her tears and said, "Yes, I most certainly did, one my father repaired for me."

Corn Crib

The corn crib slumps beside a ripened field
while twelve-row combines roar and clatter past
in clouds of swirling dust that twist across
a field of broken stalks and scattered husks.

The crib once dried whole cobs of corn for feed.
Now ears are shelled afield and blower cured
then stored in bins until the price is right
and golden kernels sell for top cash yield.

The empty crib sags low on weathered studs
as drying winds blow through its beveled slats
to hum a dirge of death in minor chords
and moan in mournful woodwind sharps and flats.

Cindy Fox *Poetry*

Unanswered Prayers

You brush away a dry tear at his funeral, just so others can see you care. You bow your head, stumble through the Lord's Prayer and sidestep its meaning.

He lived on the farmstead where he was raised, the only home he had ever known. He shied away from crowds, but he hated his solitary life even more. Too timid to approach a woman, loneliness had been his life-long companion.

Rumor said he was a rich man, one of those farmers who tucked his hard-earned dollars under a sagging mattress. In the fall of his life, he still slept in a single bed and saved bacon grease and yesterday's coffee.

The walls of his house were unadorned, no pictures of family or friends. No cookies or cakes were brought over to cheer up an aging bachelor, no signs that anyone cared.

Now, months after he has been buried, you stretch out your hands and wonder why they are empty. You bow your head while guilt and greed twist the knot tighter inside you where no one can see.

Katie Gilbertson *Fiction*

The Potatoes Only Sing When It's Raining

Old Man Caldwell was once a force to be reckoned with but time had eventually reckoned right back. Now days were spent in his small garden at his home outside St. Cloud, squatting among the potato plants. They were planted in hills, not rows. He said they would sound better that way. He explained it all to his six-year-old neighbor, Abby Mitchell.

"You see, Abby, to get potatoes to sing, you have to use only certified seed potatoes and wait till after Mother's Day to plant. Then we watch them grow and after they're done flowering, we wait three weeks, dig 'em up and begin rehearsing!"

Abby watched him lay the seed potatoes out in the sun and came over every day to watch them as they sprouted. She quivered with excitement while he finally cut the sprouted potatoes into seed, then helped by carefully setting them aside for another two days until the cuts had healed a little. Abby helped Caldwell work the soil on the two hills. It was enough room for fourteen potato plants which he said would be enough to make a fine chorus.

After the mid-May planting, Caldwell went to work on the straws. "Look, Abby," he said, "we put little holes along the length of this glass straw. Then when it's windy and rainy, the potatoes will open up their mouths and you never heard anything so beautiful! But remember the potatoes only sing when it's raining."

Abby watched as he took the little four-inch straws and drilled small holes along each one, with no two alike. This would give each potato a unique voice.

That night Caldwell wrote his sister at the retirement home.

Dear Sister:

Remember when Gramps and Gram tried to tell us that radishes could dance and how much fun we had growing radishes and making them into puppets? My little neighbor, Abby, is six years old. I told her that potatoes sing in the rain and we have lots of fun talking about it and she helped me make little flutes out of glass straws and I might actually get some kind of sound out of it. She tells me about school and the dance lessons she wants to take and I tell her about Gramps and growing radishes. She really enjoys digging around in the dirt with me and I am glad to help a little gardener along. It is something I have enjoyed all my life and maybe someday she will share it with her grandchildren. I always wanted a grandchild and when Brenda died, I thought that I would never have one but Abby is smart and friendly and reminds me a lot of Brenda.

All summer Abby helped Caldwell water the potato hills and fertilize the soil. She measured the plants each day to see how much they had grown and told her parents the potato flowers were beautiful.

Kevin Mitchell called Sheriff Anderson. "I don't think he's dangerous but he is sure off his rocker with all that talk about singing potatoes."

"OK, I'll go out and see him," said Sheriff Anderson.

Late that afternoon, Sheriff Anderson drove over to Caldwell's house and walked around to the small garden. Sure enough, Caldwell and Abby were crouched over the potato plants. As Anderson moved closer, he could hear Caldwell talking.

"Now, there you go. You will be a fine singer. Just listen to your neighbor. She will have a loud voice and you can follow right along.

And you," he said sternly, shaking his finger at another plant, "you have to stop causing trouble with your jazzy scats!" Abby laughed.

"We're just having some gardening fun, Sheriff," said Caldwell, with a wink at Abby. Since all seemed well, the sheriff left.

By mid-September, the potatoes were out of the ground and washed. Caldwell and Abby drew little faces on them.

They spent a happy late September Saturday afternoon cutting lengths of twine and inserting the glass straws into the potatoes drawn-on mouths. The tiny hole for the straw went all the way through the potato for more air flow. Then he drilled a hole at about where the fore-head would be and threaded the piece of twine through it. It was for hanging from the tree, he explained. Now they just had to wait for rain.

That night at supper, Abby's parents asked what she and Caldwell had been doing all day. Abby told them all about how the potatoes were ready to sing, but it had to rain first.

Caldwell's talk about singing potatoes might have been entertaining for a child, but her parents were uncomfortable even though they were sure he meant no harm. They kept Abby close to home.

The weather report for the night of October 2 was rain and more rain. Caldwell excitedly spent a whole day up on a ladder in the tree between his house and Abby's tying the potatoes carefully so they were all visible from any one of the Mitchells' windows.

The Mitchells looked out across the yard and saw dozens of pota-toes hanging from the tree, each with a thin glass straw coming out of where a mouth might be.

"This is too much," said Sheila Mitchell. "Kevin, please do some-thing!"

That afternoon, Sheriff Anderson drove back to Caldwell's farm to take him to the local hospital to be checked out.

"Not tonight, Sheriff, please! It's going to rain and I want to be home to hear them singing!"

"Who?" asked Sheriff Anderson.

"Why, the potatoes. I've been working on it all summer. Please."

Nothing would deter the Sheriff and the two drove off towards town with Caldwell slumped and dejected in the back seat.

That night Abby woke up to the sound of raindrops in the leaves. It was followed by another sound, faint at first. Abby was joined by her parents and they stood at the window and watched the potatoes swinging from the trees, the straws vibrating, their voices swooping and soaring over the rain.

Nothing lost,

forgotten, faded from
this graying head, I
just wanted you to
know that I still remember
all those things,
I remember your
long brown hair
hanging straight beside
those green, green eyes; how
small you were in
jeans and jacket and
how I could not stop
kissing you on those long
ago nights, could not
stop until I fell asleep
myself rather than
take you home; love
was an ache then,
something dense

within my chest—
I remember the firelight
and hot river afternoons,
all of it, when I was learning
how to touch you—
those were the
had-to-see-one-
another days, had to
hold hands and kiss
and yes I know
you think I don't
recall, but I do,
and today I wanted you to know
that I do remember, I do
and it made me
weep, pathetic old man
wiping his eyes on
the plane, remembering—

Marilyn Wolff *Poetry*

Day Care

She clings to my hand
as we enter through the large doorway.
My heels click slowly
on the tile in the hallway.
She pads along beside me.

Heads turn, eyes stare
as we pass many rooms.
We are new here.

As we move ahead
her fingers tighten on mine.
Anticipation or fear?

Will you remember to pick me up?
Of course.

Will we play games?
I'm sure you will.

Will I meet new friends?
I hope so.

We round the corner,
find the room we seek.
I give her hand a squeeze,
turn, and leave
my 91-year-old mother
at the Adult Day Care Room.

The Orchard

Richard looked out the window and took a sip of coffee from his "#1 Grandpa" mug. The sun was just reaching the top of his apple trees, and the sunlight gave the orchard a mystical glow. A letter from the City Commissioners sat ominously on the table, however, casting a very different aura throughout the kitchen. Richard tried to ignore it.

"The feeders are empty," he said, watching a Blue-winged Warbler peck at the last kernels of bird food. Even though it had been over a year since his wife had died, Richard often waited for a response. If he looked hard enough, he could still see her working in the garden, her face covered with patches of sweaty earth. He had done his best to keep the weeds out and the plants growing, but it was as if they knew he wasn't Lucy. It was the worst crop in years.

Richard finished his coffee, swallowed a bite of toast, and grabbed his coat. His appetite was fleeting at best, but he forced down the sustenance. "Let's go, Paco," he said. "Time's a wasting." Richard watched as his orange tabby came around the corner, yawning and stretching away the sleep. It sauntered across the kitchen as if entitled to the open door. Paco had been a gift from Richard's son, Tommy, soon after Lucy died.

"I don't want to worry about you," he'd said, passing the feline to Richard's reluctant arms. "Paco will take care of you, give you someone to talk to," Tommy insisted. Although resistant, Richard found himself talking to Paco by the time they had driven the fourteen miles home. *At least I'm not talking to myself,* he thought.

Richard's property was home to almost four hundred trees: apple, chokecherry, apricot. For the better part of two decades, he had cared for them with the love and tenderness that was often missing from his relationships with people. Truth be told, he liked the trees better. There was an innate peace present in the orchard that Richard was unable to find elsewhere. He felt like the trees understood him, appreciated him. Each fall, they would reward his care with fruit far sweeter than anything found in town. His family may have questioned his devotion to the trees, but they eagerly awaited the harvest.

Richard and Paco filled the bird feeders and departed on their morning stroll through the trees. Even though the sun was shining, it felt as if they knew something was amiss in Richard's world. He had yet to tell them that he was being forced off his land, that developers would soon begin construction on a flood retention wall for the city. Richard had fought tirelessly with City Commissioners and state politicians. He had even gone toe-to-toe with members of the U.S. Army Corps of Engineers. Nobody listened.

"How can I possibly replace you?" he said, running his hand along the side of an apricot tree. "They just don't understand." Since losing his wife of forty-six years, Richard had come to depend on the stability and security offered by the trees. Each morning, no matter what, he could look out his window and they would be there. No cancer. No death. His body ached when he pictured the bulldozers.

Richard continued walking deeper into the orchard, occasionally stopping to offer Paco a bite of the vanilla wafer he carried in his pocket. The air was heavier than usual and Richard had to stop more than once to catch his breath. Near the end of the chokecherry trees, his breathing became more labored and he was unable to slow down his respirations. He sat at the base of the tree, cradling Paco across his outstretched legs. The cat had adopted the old man's reclusive persona shortly after his arrival, and rarely snuggled. It must have sensed what was happening, however; Richard had heard that animals could do that. He wondered if the trees knew as well.

Richard took in as much of the orchard's sweet smell as possible. After one last look around, he leaned back, closed his eyes, and waited for Lucy.

The Truth About Rainbows

When you see a rainbow,
you still think about Father,
his laugh; all the colors
he possessed: his bold redness,
his sometimes yellow streaks

During the funeral, you stared
at his folded hands, scrubbed
fingernails, his body dressed
in a Sunday best blue suit;
the green foliage of violets,
sympathetic lavender pansies
next to the casket; you thought
about the younger man,
how he pressed when things
didn't always go well

And like the rainbow, with all its
orange and indigo, with all its fuss
and ado, its shortness of breath—

at times like these, what did
it really matter, anyhow?

Heidi Hemmer *Poetry*

Picking Tree's Bark

The willow
sweeps back and forth
massaging the air
      in the rough wind.
My hair snaggles, goosebumps
  appear on my arms.
  The grass
prickles
    below. Squirrels watch me
walk by.

Your
face is in
that tree. Silky smooth dark complexion,
Cheshire cat smile.
      Even that tree has a
      big forehead.

I wrap my arms around the trunk,
picking off bark,
tears start to
      fall.
      The squirrels shake their heads and continue
to gather nuts.

Looking for a Christmas Tree with Dad

it had nothing to do with the holiday
really a waste of trees
it was just a family thing
a tradition
that made it special
this walking through the woods with Dad
something I looked forward to all year

Dad would find his ax and his booming smiling voice
would fill up the room
Ready to go?
and we scrambled to find our boots and coats

the air was impossibly clean and cold
biting as we breathed it in
we would venture off into the woods
and he pointed out spruce trees we could choose
deer tracks and rabbit tracks crossed our path
and Dad would tell us what they were

I will always remember the way
the call of a blue jay knifed across the morning
the way Dad showed us
his love of the forest, of trees, of lumber
and told us tales of working in lumber camps
the horses with harnesses clinking in the cold

snorting frosty clouds
the hard work
the dray full of logs

it had nothing to do with the holiday
really a waste of trees
it was just a family thing
a tradition
that made it special
this walking through the woods with Dad

The Year

It was the year he didn't take the tree off the car. He'd picked out the tree the year before, as he always had—a Norway pine. She liked Norway pine for its fullness. Snow had been hip deep. He'd run clothesline through all four windows, tied it down, and rolled the windows up until only a crack of cold whistled through. He'd turned the heater way up and was warm as toast, bundled up as he was.

If she were here, she'd remember for him what year it was. But she wasn't. At least, he thought she wasn't. Or was she one of the women at his table—the one with the matted wig or the one with reading glasses dangling where her bosom used to be. Or that other one, the one who had to have her food cut up and each piece put on a fork before she'd lift it to her mouth.

He'd gone up to the house that year to ask her to hold the door open as she always had before he'd take the tree off the roof of the car. He'd rung the doorbell and then pushed on the door handle, surprised it had opened so easily. "What year was that?" he asked the ladies, for he thought of them in that polite way as ladies. "1952," the one with the wig said. The one with the reading glasses lifted them to her face and looked through them without putting them on. "She's not right," she said. The other woman chewed her mouthful of meat rapidly, as if she wanted to finish so that she could say something, but didn't.

He'd called out for her, not wanting to track on the carpet, knowing she'd be unhappy if he did. And his voice had seemed larger to him than it was, as if his words filled the living room with heavy furniture. If she were here, she'd remember for him. But she wasn't. He was sure of it. She didn't wear wigs or reading glasses or chew with her mouth open.

"It's the mill . . . illllll . . . iummm," the one with her moist mouthful said. The one with the smudged reading glasses lifted them to her face again, looked at him through them without putting them on, and said, "She's not right."

It was the year he didn't take the tree off the car, the Studebaker he thought it was. He couldn't remember why he didn't. It was the tree he'd picked out the year before, a Blue Spruce, he thought. She liked Blue Spruce for its fullness. "And its color," he said aloud to the ladies. "She'd liked it for its color." But they were stuffing their mouths like Christmas stockings.

Maybe he hadn't said it aloud. Maybe he only thought he had. So he said it again louder. And louder yet again. "Its color. She liked it for its color." And the ladies all looked up and smiled. They were ladies. He thought of them in that polite way as ladies. And if she were here, she would help him remember. And then they would both go for a drive in the country.

He would drive and she would look out the window. And he would look out her window past her, and he would say, *You couldn't tell the sky from the snowy fields if it weren't for trees.* She always liked it when he said things like that. *That's lovely*, she'd say.

The girl waiting on their table brought the dessert cart and placed a chocolate ice cream gingerbread man in front of the lady with the matted wig and a bright green Christmas tree in front of the lady with reading glasses dangling where her bosom used to be. Then returned to the cart for the other two.

She'd open the door for him whenever he came home. He loved that about her. She was an angel. "An angel," he said aloud. And then louder.

"It's a snowman," the girl said, placing another too bright Christmas tree in front of the lady with her mouth always open.

"It's an ice cream snowman," the girl said. "See his top hat."

She'd always be there to open the door. He couldn't remember when she wasn't.

Sharon Chmielarz *Poetry*

The Pillow Cleaners Come to Town

and turn the senior citizen center
into an automated assembly line.

Goodbye, dross of long winter nights.
Farewell, old skin cells and reek:

what couldn't come clean on a clothesline.
Bundles of pillows, caroming, bouncing,

sloshing along, even as more
mistresses of pillows hurry through the door,

hugging stained sacks of feathers
like thoughts kept well past prime.

Kate Halverson *Poetry Honorable Mention*

Last Rites

Tonight I wash her back
sturdy hand bars recently installed
first one, now three.

Per her request, I scratch her back
hard enough to please, the matriarch
repeatedly cooing like a baby bird—
Your father 's job, when he was alive.

An evening bath. One of life's simplest
pleasures—her weekly communion,
one lit candle large enough not to forget,
a current fashion magazine within reach.

Letting her soak alone in peace
I watch over near the door. *All done*
she announces like a two year old
finishing up a new habit learned.

Wrapping my still formidable shrinking
mother in my arms, our weekly ritual
washes away worries—momentarily.

Peeking 'round the corner, last rites
line up down the hall, arriving either
too soon—or not soon enough.

Rebecca J. Krystosek *Creative Nonfiction*

The New Smell of an Old Gun

An itch for far-flung adventure has always rendered me restless, so I didn't wait long after high school before I packed up and headed east to attend college. Born in northern Minnesota and raised a few miles from the headwaters of the Mississippi, I neither fully appreciated the natural beauty of my home nor the quirks and charms of its people. At that juncture, I was more concerned with what I was missing out on by virtue of being relegated to the woods than with what they might have to offer.

As a freshman at Dartmouth, among prep-school grads mostly from the Atlantic and Pacific coasts, I was walleye sans water. During orientation, a few clueless Californians inquired about the availability of electricity and sled dogs as a mode of transportation back home. Jaws dropped and eyes bulged at the thought of a place so rustic that deer hunting season warrants district-wide days off from school. My accent drew interest the way salt licks attract deer. At the slightest mention of my home state, classmates and colleagues would launch into exaggerated renditions of the movie *Fargo* and finally collapse into fits of self-induced laughter.

Over the intervening years, I've lived twice in New Hampshire as well as Washington, D.C., Los Angeles, Saint Louis, and Barcelona. My accent has lost most of that familiar backwoods cadence, ostensibly traceable to Native and Scandinavian tongues. I gave it up partly out of neglect and partly out of a conscious effort to leave it behind. It freed me of the ignorant questions, from the *Fargo* reenactments, from the maddening plight of being born to the middle of the country.

Given all this, it came as a surprise to my family that I quit my job in New England and moved back to the area after almost a decade away. That I wanted to hunt for the first time at age twenty-seven came as an even bigger surprise to my father, a man for whom—like so many others in this neck of the woods—hunting is more akin to a sacred ritual than a hobby or a sport. After all, I was the one who'd never touched a gun, who'd defiantly rebuffed every offer from the devoted hunters of my family—my dear old Gramps, uncle, big brother, and Pops—to teach me the delicate art of bringing home the venison.

"Really?" His head was tilted in surprise, and his eyes were wide with a mixture of skepticism and hopefulness. He paused and drew in a deep breath.

"If you really mean it, then I'm going to call your uncle. And oh, it would have made your grandpa so happy." It was only then, as I saw the corners of my Pops's sparkling eyes gather traces of moisture, that I realized just how deeply those four simple words—I want to hunt—had affected him.

As a young man, my father started hunting more as a favor to his father than out of any real desire to slay deer. In time, he grew to relish the bond they shared over three decades. It was a union formed over sacramental meals of Grandma's coffeecake and kielbasa before dawn, strenuous efforts to recover hefty deer from deep in the swampy river valley and, most of all, marathon storytelling around the fireplace long after my normal bedtime.

Grandpa was a lifelong farmer and, although nearly deaf, an epic storyteller whose tales of monster bucks, the Great Depression and Prohibition-era bootleggers colored my childhood and that one special week each November when he and his stash of Halloween candy would come to stay during Opener. Over the years, his vast repertoire of deer tales came to include big bucks and solid does that even I knew well. He was diagnosed with cancer and swiftly passed while I was studying in Spain. Even now, I can't help but wish I had heard him tell just one more yarn before, as he would have put it, he kicked the bucket and bit the dust.

The two of us made our way to the gravel pit with a homemade target a week before Opener. Pops gave me a thorough course in gun safety and showed me the ways of Grandpa's old .30-30. It was a 1943 Winchester which had served him well, even during the war years when the scarcity of ammunition relegated him to two or three shells for the whole season. As my father shared cautionary accounts of people he knew who'd forgotten to reset the safety or had left an extra shell in the chamber, my palms grew sweaty and my chest tight.

"Maybe I ought to try bow hunting instead," I ventured aloud.

"No, you've got this," he reassured me. "Just remember what I taught you and line up the bead. It shoots just a little high and to the right. Make the first shot count. Like Grandpa used to say, if you hear one shot, they got it. Two, it's a toss-up. Three shots, it definitely got away."

I took a good while to steady my aim, cock the hammer and make the first shot—my first shot ever—really count. I remember that deafening millisecond, the jolt to my cheek and shoulder, the new smell of an old gun. These foreign sensations coalesced to form a strangely familiar feeling and, without knowing precisely why, I felt at home. We walked the fifty yards to our homemade target and, with great relish, Pops examined the cluster of bullet holes.

"Not bad, not bad at all. Without a scope, too . . . you'd even give your mother a run for her money." My second and third shots came easily within a few centimeters of that first hole. "You're ready, Rebecca. I know Grandpa would be grinning." I couldn't help but smile myself at the thought of Gramps and the realization that I'd soon have a yarn or two of my own to add to his beloved tales.

Sharon Tauber *Poetry*

Away

Twelve or twenty robins tossed onto the dry grass of my backyard,
Chirruping amid the leaves cast off by waning trees,
Whorls of leaves tumbling through on the breath of the north wind,
Carried away to drop into ditches or snag in a line of brush.

It is time for me to be carried away on the wind,
Away from this sweet melancholy,
Away over the blue-grey clouds fringed with the sun's last glow,
Away to a place where long days glimmer across balmy seas.

But, no, I will stay as the days get shorter, welcoming the cold night,
For I am no longer so vibrant that I can stand all that light.
If I listen I can hear a train whistle, forlorn across flat fields of white
As I sink into sleep under the weight that blankets me.

In July

In July, heat set its intention and held to it—in a steaming aura of eye-squinting light—saturating sidewalks, slathering the city's intersections, settling a hazy mirage over storefront windows—and siphoning all energy from body, mind, and psyche.

In July, Crave Ice Cream Parlor was the busiest establishment in town. My daughters, Lissa and Lyric, could not *not* order Oreo flavor ice cream. Though, without a miss, they opted to sample the *flavor-of-the-moment*, always an "urban-theme"-named ice cream flavor, descriptors that grew more enigmatic with each passing swelter of a day: Hennepin-Avenue-Detour-Pecan, Graffiti-Rave-Sorbet, and my personal favorite: Light-Rail-Controversy-Mocha.

I longed for strawberry. Let's say I yearned for it, let's say I yearned for it like the yearning for a lost lover, that's how much. They never had it. *How could that be?*

"Seems strawberry is about as basic as chocolate, or vanilla . . ." I said to the ice cream server, a young man with an inky tattoo winding down his arm and over his wrist, elbow deep in a vat of Urban-Melt-down-Peppermint-Swirl.

" . . . can't understand why I can never find that flavor." He topped off the cone, handing the double-dipped dream to the teen next to me. Her hair matched her ice cream, which distracted me, momentarily, from my plea.

"Think of it," I said, turning back to the tattooed-one. "Strawberry ice cream . . . You could name it something like: "Strawberry-Traffic-Jam." He looked at me—raised a pierced eyebrow. "OK, Strawberry-Stalemate," I said.

I capitulated with "City-Sanscrit," a flavor I chose for the name alone. My daughters sighed into their Oreo bliss.

In July, Crave Ice Cream Parlor was a siege of summer nights' community intimacy: city folks eating ice cream at outdoor tables, close. Vines running a hush over bricked walls beneath a slither-lit evening sky. Suspended tiny lights: blue yellow green blinked over strollers pulled up snug to tables. Parents, leaning toward their children, wielding wads of napkins, wiping trailing drips of ice cream dribble from tiny fingers, chins, cheeks—barely managing the "keeping up" in the contest between tongue and *melt.* All, in the sticky evening air of a July that had decided to grace us with the most incessant heat and humidity that I could remember.

Except for the record-breaking heat in July, the summer after Lissa was born—when I was anemic, Lissa—colicky, Jess—barely two years old, and my husband, always, walking out the door.

In July, Lissa, now 22 years of age, returned, post college graduation, to live at home again for "just a few weeks," turned six months—throwing our family dynamics into all-craziness, setting Lyric to complaining that she was trying so hard not to feel "little" and with her "big sister" back in the bedroom across the hall from hers, all over again, she was feeling like the little sister all over again. And I, without a minute in the house without someone with me, talking to me, needing something. From me. Or frustrated about something-or-other. Something-or-other, with me.

In July, we all went to therapy. In every configuration that three people can mathematically add up to. And we had ice cream. All the time. On the way home from anywhere—therapy, for example—the question would invariably arise: "Anyone up for ice cream?" "Anyone" was always up for ice cream.

In August, Lissa decided that her bedroom looked like her "little girl" bedroom and spent the better part of a day changing it over in every possible way.

In August, Lyric, in one fell swoop, moved every bit of the contents of her bedroom to Jess's old room at the far end of the hall—bigger, more windows, more light; with tiny green-leafing grapevines wildly fluorescent over the screens, turning her bedroom into a treehouse.

In August, we all started to figure out how not to be so hard on one another, and . . .

In August, my anemia was diagnosed. Just like that long ago summer of those ninety-six-degrees-and-climbing, day-after-days, when Lissa was a baby, just weeks old, instead of twenty-two years. When I had no energy. At all.

In August, I wondered if I was craving ice cream because my body knew it needed nurture. Filling. And I wondered if Lissa craved being home because she needed that very thing, as well—because she missed some things, from me, when she was a baby. When I was so sick after her birth. Things I can't give her, still. Breaking my heart. All over again.

In August, I gave up looking for strawberry ice cream at Crave. Let's say I gave up on that lost lover. I had discovered Desire's-Revenge. That was the name of it: Caramel and hot fudge trailing over mounds of vanilla bean ice cream in a sultry, reckless abandon *what took me so long?*

In August, Lissa switched to Coconut Italian sodas. Lyric stayed true: Oreo.

John Thornberg *Poetry Honorable Mention*

Postcard

May arrived yesterday,
a bouquet of apple blossoms
still fresh on her breath.
A pair of robins are homesteading
the big oak beside the house,
weaving a little love nest
just above the old rope swing
where you and I first kissed.
It rained this morning, briefly,
but the sun has folded his umbrella,
and the lilacs are lined up again
at the roadside perfume counter,
comparing fragrances sprayed
on their tiny flowered wrists.
Over the fallowed fields I hear
a lonely meadowlark singing
his rendition of hearts and flowers,
just as he did the day you died.
Wish you were here.

Louise Bottrell *Creative Nonfiction*

Trains and Tractors

I climbed the gnarled old tree and scrambled onto the roof of our front porch. I carried the latest Nancy Drew book in a flour-sack drawstring bag. I could lean against the clapboard siding of the upper story and survey our big bare yard. We did not pay any attention to that yard, other than mowing it with a push mower once in a while. We took the grass for granted, along with dandelions, clover, buckhorn, and chiggers. Lots of chiggers. An oiled country road unraveled past the yard and, 100 feet beyond, the steel rails of the New York Central Railroad shimmered in the sun.

A warning whistle before the train sped through our Central Illinois town of Windsor, several miles to the east of our farmhouse, alerted me. The fast-moving passenger trains were my favorites: a fleeting glimpse of pale faces, hats and colorful clothes, and the traveling riders were out of sight, leaving me to imagine their adventures.

I liked the slower-moving freight trains, too. I could see the engineers at the controls as they rumbled by. Grandmother Maude told me a story about a pretty girl who sat on her porch swing and waved at a train engineer every day. He always waved back. Then one day, he called on the girl. He had fallen in love with her. She loved him, too. They were married and lived happily ever after.

That gave me an idea. I put on my Sunday dress, waited on the porch until I heard the whistle. We did not have a swing, so I ran into the middle of our yard. I waved and waved as the train approached, and that engineer gave me a big wave. Every time I tried that, the engineers waved back. None of them ever came to see me.

However, one of my fifth grade classmates, Jimmy Bottrell, drove his small Fordson tractor by our house almost every summer day on the way to his dad's farm. Sometimes, when he saw me in the yard, he stopped in our driveway. We talked about Saturday matinees, Harvest Picnic, or our school friends. Nine years later, Jimmy asked me to marry him and, so far, we have lived happily ever after.

Sister Kate Martin *Poetry*

Debut

When poems come they are a surprise
but they must be longed for:
eyes scanning the neighborhood,
ear cocked for a sound or a word,
the heart quizzed, as though one could
insist that it remember everything.

All this attention, this longing and sifting
and hoping that the right words will appear—
rabbits from the hat of inspiration—
O little poem, what burdens have been
laid on your frail shoulders,
before you are led out to meet the world.

Michael Kiesow Moore *Poetry*

If I Could Do It Over Again

I would carry my books like a girl.

I would cross my legs however I wanted.

When someone would hold a buttercup under my chin, I would say, "Everyone's chin looks yellow when you do that. So that means you're queer, too, right?"

I would let my wrists move however they wished, and not as if they were in straight splints.

When tested on how I look at my fingernails, I would do what comes natural and not try to remember how boys are supposed to do it.

I would speak of Tchaikovsky and Shakespeare and not pretend to know anything about sports.

When I would call out, "Sticks and stones may break my bones, but names will never hurt me," I would mean it.

I would let my mom kiss me at the front door before I head to school, and so what if someone saw.

If I could do it over again, I would live a life where eyes did not watch my every move and, if any did, I would yell, "Now watch this!"

If I could do it over again, I would wear pink and be damn proud of it.

204

John Thornberg *Poetry*

Deja Voooooo

In the night I hear the sound
of a train, and in my dream
I lean again into the rush of it,
a boy leaning into the future
as it roars by from the past.
A forbidden thrill, I wanted
to feel the blast of its breath,
breathe the sheer power of it,
breathe the spirit of this beast
that flew down the steel tracks
to its vanish point and beyond.
But now as I look back at him
from the caboose of my life,
I see only a small boy waving,
wondering what became of me.

Permanent Record

"All right, young lady, this *will be* on your Permanent Record."

Only the meanest teachers threatened you with your Permanent Record, and only the most evil of all actually wrote on it. It wasn't the same as your report card; it was some top-secret record you could never see, but knew would follow you all the days of your life.

Permanent Records exist only in tax-funded public schools because public schools require accountability. Friends from parochial schools never worried about Permanent Records; they had it easy, they only had to worry about going straight to hell.

After high school graduation I led a dodgy life of fear, certain my Permanent Record would unexpectedly appear. And, as I ventured forth into the world, I found from time to time, *it did*.

Didn't they hire someone else when I applied for my first job at White Castle? Didn't the Admissions Director from Wellesley leaf through a pile of papers, look up startled, then downright hostile? And shortly thereafter, wasn't I rejected from five Ivy League Colleges and only reluctantly accepted at the U of M?

An ever-present fear of exposure was the reason I never pursued a civil service or law career; I knew there was no point. My Permanent Record would reveal all my petty school crimes and misdemeanors. There was the time in sixth grade when I chalked huge yellow Zs on the back of Judy Rust's camelhair coat the year Zorro was my hero. And there was what came to be called the *Orange pelting incident*, where I pelted boys with fruit from an eighth grade classroom's second story window. And, most famously, the time my cooking teacher slammed down her wooden spoon, clapped her floury hands in my face, and demanded I turn in my hairnet and apron. All that and more, had been declared, by furious faculty, to be recorded indelibly on my Permanent Record.

I had no reason to disbelieve.

As I aged, finished college, and raised a family, I didn't spend *all* my time dwelling on its existence, although I did think about it when an espe-cially heinous crime was committed, and the newspaper disclosed the fact the perp "didn't mix well with others in school" or "flunked shop." I knew immediately a reporter must have had a gander at the criminal's Permanent Record.

I never knew quite how one got that peek, until an old semi-boyfriend, whom my father long ago referred to as *the greaser*, wrote our high school's alumni paper informing us all that with a small fee and a signature, our Per-manent Records were available and, it was, as he said so eloquently, "in a perverse way, a hoot to read."

I was elated by the news of all that secret information being revealed, and within the week I held in my hands my personal Holy Grail, the cause of all my problems. It existed! Three pages of test scores, academic grades, citizenship records, attendance records, SAT scores, IQ test results and in-deed, yearly teacher notes on personality, attitude and appearance.

The first surprise for me was that I am, as a woman, exactly the little girl I was in grade school. The teacher's comments, *Talks too much. Slov-enly and disorganized*, pretty much sums me up still. I babble on, my roots are showing and, as for disorganized, just try dropping in at my house unan-nounced. *Nothing's* changed.

There was one strange comment from my third grade teacher in which she remarked I dressed like a boy and acted like a boy. I suppose that has changed but I'd never trade in my tomboy stage for anything and I wonder why she felt it necessary to comment. She also checked a box which read *not normal* as opposed to the box for *normal* next to family status because someone explained to me I had a half-sister and my brother had Down syn-drome. A *normal* family in those days consisted of father, mother (married) and children who were considered healthy and hence, *normal.*

I laughed out loud at my favorite teacher comment: *The other children seem to like her.*

Happily the record wasn't completely negative. Teachers also said I loved life and was enthusiastic and happy.

Reading the details, I realized I have selective memory. I was certain I'd had perfect attendance and even possessed the much-coveted Perfect Attendance Pin. But there, on that waxy transcript paper lay the truth: *Grade 3: 11 days absent, 2 days tardy. Grade 4: 9 days absent, 4 tardy.* I could hardly believe it, as I am and was with my children, a tyrant of tardiness. As for that pin, I must have really wanted one. I swear I remember pinning it to my blouse!

I chewed out my son for his so-so ACT score and the record revealed my score to be identical. My SAT score was hundreds of points away from the nearly perfect 1600s I brag about. I used to fret that my parents might have a look at my Permanent Record but now I dread the possibility of my *children* getting a peek.

Near the end of the transcript I found two IQ Test scores, one from fifth grade and one from seventh. The fifth grade score was twelve points higher than the seventh grade score, and in seventh grade I had my first real crush on a boy. No further explanation needed! In sixth grade Miss Swanbeck said I would become an actress and, in ninth, Mr. Monte said school teacher. Both were forgetting, of course, with my Permanent Record trailing me, I would never be hired by anyone.

And as for all those dreadful things I did which they threatened so often to put in my Permanent Record? They weren't there. The job I didn't get at the White Castle must have been a sixteen-year-old girl's bad interview skills, all those college rejections no doubt the mediocre SATs, and as for my unrealized career? The *Orange pelting incident*, indeed.

Bob Sullivan *Poetry*

Under the Clouds

Stay under the clouds
Lest we discover what lies above them

Stay under the clouds
Where you can hold her in your arms
And still cherish the moment

Stay under the clouds
For fear that it will all disappear

Stay under the clouds
Where so many need so much from so few
And enough is never enough

Stay under the clouds
Where perfection is unattainable
Yet we continue to strive
Even though happiness is elusive

Stay under the clouds
The clouds are as high as you can reach
After that can only be glory

Laura K. Murray *Creative Nonfiction*

Saints

I decided to be a saint early on.

Saints had whole days named just for them and their own full-page spreads in my Children's Book of Saints. Even after dying horrible deaths in the name of God, their bodies remained perfect, just like Snow White's in her glass coffin. They had rays of sunshine through their mosaicked faces, testifying to their unbreakable, unshakable faith.

I loved sitting below the church windows on sunny mornings, feeling the colors pour warm over my head, knowing my hair was radiating green or red. "Doesn't she look just like an angel?" I was sure they whispered in the pews behind us.

I wanted to be like Bernadette, whose pale face was outlined in my book by a semi-circle of yellow goodness, who saw a lady in white with roses growing straight out of her feet.

Or Cecilia, with her flowing hair and creamy complexion and sugary voice that could lull you into sleep or even heaven. They locked her in a sauna and flipped the dial all the way to the right so that her fingernails just about melted off. When they tried to cut off her head, she just kept singing even as her spirit began to leave her body.

Grandma stacked the hats and mittens in clear plastic bags for the poor Indians, a careful seventy-five counted into each.

"They're little girls just like you, you know," she told me. "It gets so cold, they need something to keep their poor hands warm."

I wondered what the poor Indians thought when they saw Grandma and Grandpa bouncing up the road in their big pickup truck. It was probably like Christmas, I thought.

I imagined Grandma would jump down and snap open the back of the truck bed. The littlest ones would surround Grandpa in their bare feet and my jeans from last year, and one shy girl with a long black braid would grab onto his jacket cuff because little kids do that with Grandpa. Maybe it was how his blue trucker cap sat just a bit high on the top of his head or the way his eyes twinkled when he laughed. "Richard Dreyfuss," said the woman who brought him Communion in the hospital after his heart surgery. "That's who he looks like. Yep, it's the sparkly eyes."

I wondered if the poor Indians even cared that Grandma spent every spare second making those mittens for them so their fingers wouldn't turn blue and fall off on their way to school. I wondered if they lived in teepees and made dreamcatchers like the one my brother had made for me at camp. I never asked.

Watching my grandparents was a parable I knew by heart, built on German work ethic and Irish devotion. I tied together their examples of love and hung the loop around my neck like a rosary chain, a reminder that some things were just as simple as they seemed, and some things were faith.

Aside from Grandpa's surgery, my grandparents were medical marvels into their eighties, their cabinets void of even Tylenol. When we drove out to Idaho one spring, Grandma raced me up the steps to Devil's Tower and won. Cancer snuck up one day just as we noticed the tiredness in her smile, the bones protruding on her arms.

She laughed at my brother's scruffy chin as he hugged her goodbye, said she thought she'd hire me as I massaged her hands, her skin like waxed paper over veins. She smiled through the needles and the nurses who turned the dials all the way to the right, smiled as her spirit began to leave her body, then struggled to sit up to give a knitted hat to the priest who briefly waved his hand over her before continuing the story of his trip to Rome.

In high school Spanish class, we were each supposed to make an altar for *el Dia de los Muertos*, the day Mexican cultures make altars for their dead loved ones and celebrate in graveyards, leaving out favorite foods and beverages for the spirits' journeys.

I don't remember how I heard about the Amish schoolhouse shooting. Mrs. McGee might have turned on the classroom TV as they had on September 11. Or maybe my mom told me the way she shared stories about parents who kept their children in cages or women who were murdered walking their dogs, as she tried to lessen the black feeling in her stomach by sharing it.

I imagined the boys getting to run out the door, a confused little girl fleeing with them unnoticed, the girls arranged in front of their lesson on the chalkboard, a 180-degree line of black tights. When I heard how two sisters offered to be shot instead of the others, I wondered if my rosary would have given me as much courage as their white bonnets had given them.

The same day, the Amish community publicly forgave the milkman with the nine millimeter. I couldn't believe it. Would they have been so quick to forgive if it had been their sons? It seemed everyone was forgetting the girls before knowing them in the first place. Maybe some people didn't deserve forgiveness.

I wondered if the girls had been like me. They must have disobeyed their parents. Maybe one of them liked to write stories, one wondered what it would be like to be kissed, one had two best friends, one was getting a sore throat.

I made my altar for them, adding bread and homespun cloth, along with my rosary. I wrote out their names: Naomi Rose Ebersol, Marian Stoltzfus Fisher, Anna Mae Stoltzfus, Lena Zook Miller, and Mary Liz Miller. I set out crayons, pencils, and paper, a textbook, cough drops, a charm bracelet, a teddy bear, and a handful of daisies. I wanted people to remember them as individuals, as brave girls.

I wanted people to know they had all been saints.

James Bettendorf *Poetry*

How Shall I see this Spring Day?

—*for Kayleen Larson (2003-2013)*

A blind man struggles along a cracked sidewalk,
his cane tap-tapping right
and sweeping left;
people step aside.
A day remarkably unlike any other,
yet not any different:

Flowers crack the earth to begin a delicate rise,
trees begin to bud, pollen heavy in the green air.
Grass awaits spring's first mow, a blessed rain
prayed for in near-empty churches
falls.

Fathers push brooms in garages
mothers wipe runny noses.
I should have been breathing the scent
of magnolias and lilacs.
I look out from behind the glass
in a skyway over Chicago Avenue,
the air smells of lemon and ammonia.

My thoughts are upstairs, in a hospital bed,
with the quiet child,
who two weeks ago showed me how fast
her new running shoes helped her fly
up the street laughing.
Now besieged by leukemia,
tubes in her nose
arm and stomach.

Her spring remarkably
unlike any other.

Deb Nelson *Creative Nonfiction Honorable Mention*

The First Dress

The store was a maze of white satin, ivory tulle, and mirrored surfaces scrubbed free of smudges. Gentle music played overhead—soothing sounds designed to drown out the buzz of fluorescent lights. A saleslady hovered, primed with exactly the right words to say. Eighteen reflections grinned back at her, each as crocodile sharp as the last.

Lisa walked from the dressing room in the first of many dresses for the day, unable to stop herself from running her hands over the smooth, white fabric. It flowed like water through her fingers. Keeping her eyes firmly on her chipped toenails, she stepped in front of one of the mirrors and onto a small platform. Only then did she look up.

"Gorgeous," cooed the saleslady, her fingers picking at the edges of the gown to make it look slightly better. "Look at your figure!"

There was a hum from the side and quiet chatter from Lisa's parents. Ignoring them, she gazed at her reflection. Her hair was a mess, the large bruise on her arm dark under the lights. The dress was pretty, though. She'd never seen herself in a long gown before. It covered her knobby knees and twisted feet.

She reached up to brush at her hair, patting it down into place. A smile pulled at the corners of her lips. She twisted her hips from side to side—almost not enough movement to be seen—and watched the silky fabric react.

Her father's heavy voice speared through, breaking her reverie. "Don't you think her shoulders look bony in this? What about a dress with sleeves?"

Lisa's gaze shifted from her reflection to the other people in the mirror. On one side of the platform her parents were seated, dressed in the best their small closet had to offer. On the other was her fiancé. Having managed to find a pair of jeans without holes, he'd added a plaid shirt stained with tractor oil.

"We pulled a dress with cap sleeves. We can definitely try it next," the saleslady said. "What do you like about this one?" She didn't even bother to look at Lisa as she smoothed out a wrinkle in the short train.

"The fabric is nice," her mother said blandly. Dark circles curled under her eyes and she clutched at a worn purse in her lap. "Satin?"

"Charmeuse satin," the saleslady agreed. "A polyester blend. It makes for an affordable alternative to silk. Isn't it beautiful?"

Lisa's father crossed his arms over his chest. His suit jacket pulled at the seams, a small handkerchief from Grandpa's funeral still tucked into the pocket. Deep-set lines surrounded the frown on his face. "I don't like this one; she looks too tall and bony. Find a dress that makes her shorter—one that's not so white." He snorted. "This is definitely not it."

Not listening, Lisa tipped her head to the side and tried to imagine herself walking down the aisle of a church. She could see it—but just barely. A looming shadow escorted her, fingers tight around her arm. A dying rose lay on the front pew, small and broken. Light shone from the head of the aisle, ready to steal her away from the darkness.

She couldn't help the smile that appeared on her face. Freeing her twining fingers to run over the dress again, she met her fiancé's eyes—blue into brown—and saw the glow that lived inside him. The small smile on his face. Warm bubbles collected near her heart.

"I like this one."

Startled by the sound of her own voice, the imagined world vanished like it had never been. Lisa froze. The lights buzzed overhead in an endless drone. Darkness clawed at the corners of the mirrors.

Her father stood in a scraping of chair on wood. Shadows cowered at his feet. His shoulders nearly burst from his black jacket, his chin held high. The mirrors lent him a flock of fallen angels. "Lisa."

Lisa ran a hand over her arm, eyes downcast. Her fingers brushed the sensitive bruise on her forearm.

"Mr. Stentson." It was nothing more than her father's name. Lisa followed her father's gaze. Her fiancé sat in his chair, calm and relaxed, but there was tension in his shoulders.

Her father stood still. The harsh lights made a fading black eye stand out against an otherwise pale face. "We agreed you could come with only if you remained absolutely silent," her father growled as he settled down into the chair.

In the quiet that followed, all eyes turned back on Lisa. "Perhaps we should try on another dress," the saleslady said, her voice uncertain.

"One with sleeves," her mother added, patting her husband's arm gently. "Her shoulders are rather bony."

"Come along then, dear," the saleslady said, leading the way back towards the dressing room. She only glanced back once.

Lisa nodded, but she stayed where she was a few moments longer, feeling brave enough to swish her hips a couple times and watch the fabric sway. She caught the grin and the small wink from her fiancé. "I like this one too," he mouthed.

The pawnshop ring on her finger glittered in the lights, catching on her reflection in the mirrors. Just for a second, all she could see were herself and her fiancé, echoed back in on themselves a million times over in a world polished free of smudges of shadows.

Then her father coughed and barked out, "You keep an eye on the price tag."

She stepped off the pedestal and headed back towards the dressing room. A dozen more beautiful gowns awaited—but she knew she'd already chosen her dress.

Ryan W. Keller *Poetry*

Minnesota Starship

All Aboard!
Minnesota Starship prepares to depart;
four-wheel drive engaged,
seatbelts cinched tight,
oh-shit handles secured;
                    icicles hang from my beard.

Windshield meteors streak by,
snowball stars moving at warp speed.
Out the side window, ghost trees
stand stripped of green and sullied,
                    busied by wind, and buried.

Windows are finally defogged enough
to redirect some heat to the feet.
Plastic floor mats hold gravel-soup,
drop a wax gas-station doughnut, turn up the heat,
                    hot chocolate gravel-soup, ready to eat.

Hazards include, *I have a big truck* fever
and a wipeout montage from the sports-car bobsled.
But the true weapons of fear are ditch missile deer,
and a black ice I.E.D. packed into a pothole bed.
                    Keep the tires full and the horses fed.

When the starship departs its cement and rafter dock
it becomes the magnifying glass helping take stock.
On days we plug it in to warm the engine block,
and snow threatens to bind us in a lock,
                    we climb aboard thankful not to walk.

Niomi Rohn Phillips *Creative Nonfiction*

Thirteenth Summer 1953

Everything changed that summer. No more wiling away the long, hot days playing hopscotch and riding bikes with my friend Antoinette. We were old enough to work. She had to take care of her little sisters and brother. I had a baby-sitting job on a farm.

I could daydream through the boring care of a baby and a toddler, but helping Teresa Schaan wash milk separators and mounds of dirty dishes in the hot, fly-filled kitchen sullied my storybook illusions about marriage and living in the country. Just the winter before I'd taken care of the baby in Teresa and Johnny's apartment in town and mooned over them all dressed up for the Saturday night dance. They came home fondling each other, anxious for me to leave. Now there was another baby, and they'd taken their place on "the folks" farm

Previous summers Antoinette and I spent lazy afternoons biking country roads, baskets packed with jelly sandwiches wrapped in waxed paper and nectar in quart jars. Now my precious Schwinn, tenth birthday gift from Grandpa, was abandoned in the tool shed.

I abandoned Grandpa and Grandma that summer, too. Ordinarily, I walked the four blocks from our apartment to their house every day. If Grandma was making *kuchen,* I stayed for supper. Grandpa entertained me with tall tales, illustrating with cartoon drawings on a yellow lined tablet. After supper we played Chinese checkers. Grandpa always cheated. Grandma always chided with a smile, "Oh, Anton."

If Grandpa was reading when I got there, Grandma helped me with crocheting. Grandpa was the only man I knew who read books—"Westerns." He didn't care for Mom's Book of the Month Club novels, but they shared copies of Louis L'Amour.

Although Grandpa had only attended school through eighth grade, he tutored me in math. "You're lucky," he'd remind me. "I could only go to school the few months between fall harvest and spring planting."

When Antoinette and I reminisce about that time, she confesses jealousy of my grandpa. Hers was old, crotchety, and barked at her when she made obligatory visits.

"Did you know he was the town drunk?" I ask. She dismisses the question with, "All those German Russian men drank a lot."

My mom might agree with Antoinette, but that didn't make her less embarrassed about Grandpa. Mom worked at Andy's Tavern on Saturday dance nights, and I overheard her tell Dad that she was "mortified" when she saw the tab Andy kept for Grandpa. But she never talked to me about it, and I never told her that he had a bottle of schnapps in his Hudson. "Just a nip," he'd wink. "No need to tell *Grossmutter.*"

Sometimes on payday Grandpa cashed his check at Andy's and treated the men sitting at the bar. If he didn't come home for supper, Grandma sent me to Andy's. It was a dark, mysterious, man's place. On a hot summer day, the cool air and smell of beer met me like a big breath when I opened the door. I'd peer into the dark. Andy would see me. "Hey, Tony. Your kid's here."

We'd walk home holding hands. Grandma would meet us at the door, muttering and scolding in German. He'd give me a silly grin and let her push him down the hallway to the bedroom. Her head barely reached his shoulder, but he never lifted a hand against her.

The summer I turned thirteen, Mom's sister, Frances, brought her husband to North Dakota to meet the family. Aunt Fran visited infrequently. Mom made remarks about her "honoring us with her presence." I wanted to grow up to be just like her—leave Balta, work at the Bon Marche in Seattle, have painted nails, and wear high-heels to work.

I got up early that morning and waited at Grandma and Grandpa's house for Aunt Fran and her husband to arrive. They finally drove up in a big black car with fins, a silver-winged woman hood ornament, and chrome bullets on the bumpers. "Cadillac Seville," Dad mumbled.

Aunt Fran opened her door and stepped out. She hugged me. "You're all grown up." Then she turned to the driver emerging from the chrome-draped car. "This is your uncle Robbie."

I saw Gordon MacCrae. His long-sleeved shirt was open at the neck, the cuffs rolled up. He wore tan dress trousers and white shoes. I'd never seen a man like him except in the movies. And he informed us, without a hint of humor, that he'd "never seen anything like this flat, treeless prairie."

"Robbie asked, 'Is this it?' at every town from the Montana border," Aunt Fran gushed. "And when we turned off the paved highway, he said, 'Is this really a town?'"

I was glad they were staying at Grandma and Grandpa's house. He might never have to know we didn't have indoor plumbing in our apartment.

Mom, Dad, Aunt Fran, and Uncle Robbie were sitting around the kitchen table. I sat on the floor, leaning against the counter, fascinated with this new uncle and, as always, entranced by Aunt Fran. Grandma was bustling around the kitchen making supper. I glanced at the red plastic teapot clock on the wall. It was past five. Grandpa was late.

I heard his first step on the porch, then an eternity between each of the next four steps. *Hail Mary full of grace* . . . He opened the door and staggered in grinning. I didn't look at Mom or Grandma. I waited for the scold in a German-English duet. No one uttered a word.

I could get up and run out of the room crying. I'd played that distract-ing role before. A protest of loyalty. It didn't faze Mom, but Grandma al-ways sympathized "Ya, Niomi . . . so sensitive. You always stand up for him." I sat there with my back pressed against the cupboard, tears rolling down my cheeks. For the first time, I knew Mom and Grandma's humili-ation.

Justin Watkins *Poetry*

Driving to Decorah in Late February

Fillmore County slides by at the window
Everywhere evidence of its layers:
Snow over soil over bedrock
Ancient ocean floors
There was saltwater here

The sun comes inside
I squint through it
Outside it is eating snow
There have been countless springs
And I know I'll never leave this place

We count nine hawks
Mostly big red-tails
Perched in majesty
Wind touching breast feathers
The oldest coats of arms

They watch from pinnacles
Not heeding roads or cars
Studying Earth's curvature
As the white rinds are
Peeled from their fields

Linda M. Johnson *Creative Nonfiction*

Keeper of the Clippers

The style is male-pattern baldness. I'm not a barber but give me a pair of clippers, a number one attachment, and I'm all set. I've seen the procedure hundreds of times.

Dad grabbed his case containing clippers, attachments, a comb. We'd drive to the farm, turning the car around in the gravel drive. The dog would thump her tail on the porch in greeting. We'd walk into the kitchen filled with warmth from the woodstove, Grandma and Grandpa, my great-aunt Ailie and my two bachelor uncles who would come in and out for coffee and visiting. And haircuts.

Dad would grab the stool from next to the stove and set it in the middle of the red and gray tiled floor. I'd be sent to the dresser at the end of the hall for the old sheet they used to cover shoulders. Male pattern baldness for all, neatly trimmed in varying shades of brown to gray.

They took turns: first Grandpa, then Sonny, then Glenn. Dad would cut hair, trim necks, go after stray hair in the ears. I'd sweep clippings and brush them into the battered metal dustpan kept behind the woodstove and dump the hair into the fire. I learned early how to carefully grab the handle and carefully tip the stovetop up. The whole time there was conversation about weather, cows, relatives. Usually in that order. Grandma, temporarily ousted from her domain between the stove and the counter, sat at the table and nipped sheets of sugar into homemade cubes until the two-handled red sugar bowl was filled.

The kitchen was the hub of the farm. By the time Dad finished, a fresh pot of coffee had been cooked atop the fire side of the stove that was half-fire, half-electric. It was a stainless pot that forced water up from below into a waiting reservoir fitted on top where grounds had been placed. Then it trickled down through the grounds into the pot. It was the best tasting coffee I've had before or since. We'd fill our cups and visit more until it was time to go. Even as a kid, I'd have coffee too.

For years, Dad kept up the routine of cutting hair. After his retirement, I took over the haircuts during winters when Dad basked in Texas sunshine. Grandma and Grandpa were gone so I only had to cut the hair of my two uncles. Ailie would still be in and out of the kitchen and we'd still do lots of visiting. By that time, I was also entrusted to cut Dad's hair during the months he was home.

Many years later. Uncle Sonny and Great-Aunt Ailie are gone now. Dad, too. Glenn lives alone on the family farm. He must be lonely, though people stop by and he does go to town now and again. But it's been years since milking cows in the barn twice daily.

Well into his eighties, he still cooks mostly on the fire side of the stove. He has a rotary dial telephone in stark contrast to the flat screen TV. "I should have gotten a bigger television," he once said. I laughed.

I bring him dinner sometimes, fixing a plate from our family's meal and dropping it by. When I visit the next time and collect my plate or plastic containers, I ask him how it was. "Oh, I ate it," he'll say. He's not being rude, just simply a man of few words. We talk about the weather, how his current dog barks until he pours her milk, how he can't walk very well anymore.

One day I made a batch of cardamom bread, the sweet bread our family has simply called biscuit. As I was mixing, kneading, baking, I thought of Glenn. How the ghosts and memories of family must linger there in the kitchen. Lone patriarch now of the family farm, his spot is on the stool parked between the stove and the counter. I brought him a loaf, still slightly warm, and told him he'd have to let me know how it turned out as I was new to bread making,

The next time I stopped, we talked about winter winds and lack of snow. I asked him how he liked the biscuit. I expected his normal, unassuming response of "It was OK."

Instead, a smile broke across his face like the sunshine streaming in through the kitchen window. "It was like Ma used to make," he said. No more had to be said. Praise in its purest, highest form.

I'm now the sole keeper of the clippers. When I go to the farm, Glenn is always in the kitchen. It gives me a jolt every time because even in the house, he wears Dad's jacket from the mill. It has Dad's name embroidered on the front and his years of service. The blue eyes, the round face. The gray hair rimming the sides of his head, the few stray hairs on top.

The routine hasn't changed. Move the stool to the middle of the floor, wrap the sheet around shoulders, secure with a safety pin, trim the ears, the neck, even a stray eyebrow.

Brush off the collar, shake the sheet off the front porch, sweep gray into the battered metal dustpan and dump into the woodstove. Except now he's down to his last cord of wood. We've been filling the woodbox in the hall for him as he can't do it anymore. He hasn't ordered more. Says he doesn't want to burden anyone to split and stack and haul wood.

So much is the same and yet so much has changed. Once that last fire has been built, a way of life that has warmed the hub of the farm will be done. But I can't bear to think about that now.

Instead, give me a pair of clippers and a number one attachment. After I'm done, let's have a cup of coffee and talk about the weather.

Jamee Larson *Poetry*

Visiting Lombardi

You slide into the worn leather chair,
a wisp of a smile breaking through your
stoic walls.

> You trace the edge of the old oak desk,
> Vince's Xs and Os reflecting off
> the respect in your eyes.

You admire the picture behind you,
the idol that has lived inside you
since you were a child.

> The realization of a dream,
> half-boy half-man
> basking in the spirit of a legend.

You visit your hero.
As I watch mine.

This Story Makes My Ass Tired

J. F. Powers. Do you know the name? He was an acclaimed American author, a recipient of Guggenheim and Rockefeller fellowships and a National Book Award winner in 1963 for his novel, *Morte D 'Urban.* He was also my mentor, a teacher of Creative Writing at St. John's University in Collegeville, Minnesota, until his death in 1999.

In 1991 I enrolled in a course he taught—Creative Writing II. I'd done well in Creative Writing I, primarily writing poetry, but also a short story my teacher had liked. It seemed logical to take the next step so I gave him a call. He did everything he could to discourage me. Without ever seeing a word I'd written, he told me I couldn't write and that I would never be a writer. He said there was no chance in hell I could write anything that would satisfy him and that he would show no mercy in his criticism of my work. He told me he was brutally honest and that he'd brought many a student, male and female, to tears with his critiques.

Well, hell, I thought, I'm as tough as that old goat. I was no traditional college student. I was thirty-nine years old, had been in the Army and been through the recent deaths of my parents. I could handle a little criticism. So despite his warning, I signed up for his one-on-one tutelage. His only requirement was forty pages of new fiction over the course of a semester—a breeze, I thought.

I began to write. My first piece failed to impress him, to put it very mildly; and neither did my second or third. I was frustrated but I doggedly kept pen to page. Fall became winter and I'd still failed to please the man except for an occasional sentence or phrase that he thought was OK.

During this time, Mr. Powers's wife, Betty Wahl, herself a published writer, was dying. He spent his days and nights caring for her and

I felt guilty about even bothering him with my futile attempts at fiction. But he insisted that I keep working and seeing him for my weekly critique.

I thought I'd reached the end of my rope one Saturday in January. We were scheduled to meet early afternoon. It had snowed all night and into the day. The wind picked up and it became bitter cold. I called J. F. and asked if I should come over to St. John's for our meeting, hoping he'd say no. But he said it was up to me. So, like a fool, I told him I would brave the snow, thinking he'd at least be impressed by my determination. I drove the five miles on unplowed country roads, glad that my old Ford had four-wheel drive. I trudged up the steps of Engel Hall where he had his office, one desk and two chairs in the building's musty attic of exposed roof beams and wall studs. The wind seemed to blow right through the walls.

I hadn't gotten to the top of the steps or even unbuttoned my coat before he said, "This story makes my ass tired!" Our session went straight downhill from there. He tore apart my story word by word, sentence by sentence. Again he told me I would never be a writer. I was wasting my time. I sat there, unable to argue, and took it for an hour before he finished with me. Then he asked if I was coming back next week. I told him yes.

The drive home was downright scary, the wind and snow having worsened. I had a hard time seeing the road at times. I cursed him at the top of my lungs as I plowed through the snow. When I finally got home, I just sat on the couch and stared out the window at the bleak winter landscape, alternately brooding and cussing. I hardly talked to my wife for two days, I was so mad and frustrated. What in hell did he want?

The following week, after I had recovered somewhat, I wrote another story and mailed it to him. During this week, his wife passed away. Two weekends later, we met again. As I drove to Collegeville, I kept asking myself why I was putting myself through this. I took a deep breath inside the door of Engel and began the climb. I felt like I was climbing the steps of a gallows!

This time he greeted me with "You just might be a writer." I was shocked. He said my story, written in the voice of an abused black woman, had floored him. I didn't know what to say. The story was littered with four-letter words and graphic violence. When I wrote it, I was at my wits' end trying to figure out how to please the man. At that point, I thought, what does it matter what I show him? He won't like it anyway. What have I got to lose?

Unfortunately, I was unable to duplicate that performance for the remainder of the semester. Nonetheless, based on that one good story, I received an "A." This was significant, but meaningless. J. F. Powers showed me how difficult writing is. I learned where I had to get mentally and spiritually and what I had to give to writing—everything.

J. F. Powers has since joined his beloved wife in the place writers go. He once told me he was happy if he wrote one good sentence a day! I had to think about that long and hard, but now I finally understand.

John Thornberg *Poetry*

The Poet Tree

I chose to write poems because
I had supposed it to be useful,
a way to talk of life and death
as partners in dancing shoes,
rather than a trudge in prose.
But all I found were rabbit trails
winding through the underbrush
laced with sparkled spider webs
dewy in the bluish hues of sunrise,
words that needed cutting back
just to see the path more clearly.
The trails fan out like branches,
full of possibilities, never coming
to a point, with tiny birds perched
nervously about, all ready to fly
without ever finishing a thought.
And at night the owl always asks,
Who, who said you could write?

Laura L. Hansen *Fiction*

The Night Journey

As we come over the ridge, the valley is a deep dark bowl below us. We feel the void. The valley has no boundaries of its own, just these softly moonlit hills that bob in and out of the cloud cover like a train of camels circling. The headman lifts an arm then, satisfied, nods for us to continue.

The beasts keen forward and with heavy feet they begin the journey down into the valley. We follow tracks that only the beasts can see, or perhaps they travel with eyes closed down paths they've traveled many times before. They huff and snort in the dark. No one speaks.

Though these hills—from a distance—seem gentle, softly rounded and green, the track we follow is littered with scree which occasionally kicks loose and scatters down the slope ahead of us sounding like the hard patter of rain. We are lulled by the quiet sure movement—down, slowly down—that continues for nearly an hour as the moon slips imperceptibly to the west.

We begin to see pinpricks of light scattered ahead, small half-hidden fires, which dance across the night valley like fireflies. Soon we hear reedy voices in ones and twos, tinninating and rhythmic, but coming from no particular source.

By now the beasts that carry us are warm with exertion and steam rises from their flanks as we pass through one rocky crevice after another, cool rock meeting heated breath, vapors rising as if from gently stoked flames. The voices we heard earlier are now closer. There is occasional laughter that comes to us with a hollow ring as if from a rock-walled grotto or pool. Again the headman raises his grizzled sinuous arm and we halt. "Here," he tells us. "We walk now." Young men come and tether the animals as our legs adjust to the ground once again. We gather in a state of confused expectation.

On foot now, we follow a labyrinthine path, shoulder-narrow, that angles sharply up to what turns out to be a series of small caves lit from inside by crude lamps and smoldering campfires. We peer inside, trying not to startle the occupants who flit between the walls like tiny bats, but who are—in fact—waif-like girls with protruding night eyes and thin black hair. They wear simple shifts that flow like diaphanous gauze but are the color of simple brown paper bags. As they move, the elfin girls seem to barely touch the cave floor with their stick-thin legs and feet. At the sight of us, there is a group startle. They shudder then still almost as one.

At the center of the cave is a round of stone benches, a council fire of sorts, and there sits a girl—tiny, tiny—with a large bound book, weathered and mildewed, that she balances on her knees and holds in barely big enough hands. This is what we have come for . . . this is what we came to see—to witness. So it is true. These are the legendary keepers of the words, the ones that tell and retell the stories that keep the world turning.

We settle in the dark outer edges of the council circle, lean against damp walls, crouch on our haunches and wait for the reading to wash over us. As we settle, the general disturbance that we created on our arrival calms, the little peeping noises of the startled gathering cease and the keepers—some seated and some moving slowly, lightly—circle the current reader. They emit low clicking sounds and a constant appreciative hum. The effect is like being in the center of a hive of bees.

The book seems to contain endless stories, words both ancient and modern. It is akin to a well-ordered book of Babel, containing something of all human language. It is more than we can comprehend in twenty lifetimes and yet, these diminutive young girls are alive with it. They are singly-purposed for this one thing.

We would stay here until our joints locked up, until we starved our own bodies to fill our minds, if we could, but the headman has stepped in—a torch in his raised hand—and his eyes appeal to us to come away. We reluctantly rise and file out into the big wordless void of the world.

Kristin F. Johnson *Poetry*

The Passion of the Dancers

(for Amanda and Antonio)
The salsa dancers forge foreheads
and linger
with fingers fit together, eyes closed.
Their feet glide to the merengue,
while everyone else watches
with envy.

Richard Fenton Sederstrom *Poetry*

Our Hands

The exactitude of execution an ancient artist
employs in the details of a bird,
titanium sheen delineated—

and yet we still have trouble depicting hands
(faces too but that is of course)
that are not complicated appendages. So why?

The hand of a young woman over there by the lake
stops painting, brush in midair.
She looks beyond her brush and a wing of fingers.

She seems to look somewhere over the water.
The hand with its brush moves out beyond her attention.
Ah. That's why. The young dancer

knows her moves, watches each part of her body
work in no more than mechanical exactitude. Then her left hand
moves by itself and she follows the grace of it.

Marlys Guimaraes *Fiction*

Lonesome Highway

"Do you want your coffee black?" the waitress with the word "Dreamer" tattooed on her neck asks me.

"No, brown, please," I answer.

She looks at me, confused. I decide 6 a.m. is too early for a discussion on the color of coffee, so I smile and say, "No cream."

My tiger-orange laptop case brushes against the olive corduroy fabric that snugs my thighs. I refuse to respond to the computer's addictive call for opening until I have had a cup of coffee.

My stomach lurches when my fingers stick to the plastic menu. I grab an alcohol wipe out of my purse to clean foreign menu matter off my hands. Road cravings of an omelet filled with hash browns, onions, green pepper and cheese wither instantly.

A white china cup, coffee filled, is placed beside a plate of dry toast in front of me.

"Jelly?" Dreamer asks, when setting a bowl of Kraft prepackaged sweets onto the table. I wanted to say, "No, I think I have enough jam on my hands from touching the menu," but remembered my manners.

Heavy boots walk across the black and white checkered, mop-streaked floor. I hear keys rattle with each step. I turn and look—just in case there really is a Marlboro man, then quickly return to studying my coffee. I am from Minnesota where it is not nice to stare.

Muscle man slides into the seat across from me. Crossed arms on the tabletop, a hearty grin, and a low hello greet me. I can't respond. I don't know how.

I move closer to my laptop, as if it is my protector, still not saying anything.

"Mind if I join you?" Blue eyes twinkle.

I am out of the booth before the eyes have a chance to twinkle twice. I almost bump into Dreamer, toss $10.00 on the counter and hurry out.

"Hey, hey you," a deep voice calls as I jump into my yellow Volkswagen parked beside an Ace Hardware semi-truck.

I think about movies where the car doesn't start at crucial moments and am grateful that the engine grinds momentarily. Suddenly I see muscle man running toward my car. Gravel spins as I pull out. I hear a fist pound on my trunk, and see a hand pointing to the back of my car.

I waver between fear and curiosity, then hit the lock button, stop my car, and crack the window. My foot sits lightly on the gas pedal, ready to trounce if need be.

"Yes?" I question as I peep out the window.

"Lady, I just wanted to tell you that your gas cap is loose and dangling." Blue eyes twinkle at me.

I look in my side mirror and sure enough, the gas door is open, a black plastic lid flops below it.

I am ashamed of myself. Here someone was being kind and helpful. How could I be so rude, so mean?

I yell, "Thanks," out the window, slam my foot on the gas pedal and fly down the road.

"Rude and mean is better than dead," I think. "I'll fix the cap later, after I am well away from Mr. Might-Be-a-Mass-Murderer."

I turn on public radio. Bach's Mass in B Minor calms me. My GPS alerts me to turn at the next exit. Twenty-five more miles and I will meet my online lover for the first time. I smile.

Moon Dreams

The moon breaks apart,
silvery shards swirl into
shadowy alcoves.
Warped fragments spin
down narrow alleyways,
ricochet off black rooftops,
fill empty streets.
Darkness gradually
dwindles to rosy dawn
and the sky spills
handfuls of blazing light.
Adrift in the past,
she edges her dreams
with tiny bits of lace.

Marilyn Wolff *Poetry*

A White Rainbow

The air was heavy with humidity and heat
the conditions just right
to create the white rainbow in the western sky,
a rarity.

We both saw it, my husband and I.
It lasted in the heavy air for several minutes.

He saw it as a sign—a promise of restoration.

It spoke to me of endings and new beginnings.
I read it right.

Sharon Harris *Fiction*

Weekend River Walk

The sun and the wind tickle the leaves and reach through to scatter dark and light. The long evening shadows send fingers of shade reaching across the river to the waving grass on the riverbank.

Two people stroll along the river, taking their habitual weekend walk. There was a time out walking that they always had to touch each other, arm in arm, an arm slung over shoulders, or hands held.

She wonders what he will say or if, as usual, he will just be silent. She will have to bring it up—his absences, the missing hours. It can't all be work. Her throat closes on the words. Why doesn't he touch her anymore? She aches for him, to have him reach for her. She feels empty and wonders when things changed.

He wonders why she never talks to him anymore. When he comes home, exhausted, she turns her back. He wants to tell her about his day, needs her encouragement for a job that is draining him. She is angry about something and he doesn't know what. He is afraid to reach for her hand now, not sure of her response. He feels lost and wonders when things changed.

They walk on, with similar thoughts locked in separate minds, hearts hardening, into the deepening shadows. They follow the musical curve of the river that they don't see or hear.

Thomas C. Stetzler *Poetry*

Alone by the Water

October sun sets low
Over Blueberry Lake
Reflecting red over the
Entire body of water.
I stop fishing to consume
The moment, stunned by
This transfiguration—this
Sacrament set so starkly
Before me. The sun stalls
On the horizon.
I watch, then, as it sets,
Listen as small lives lift
Their hymns to the stars.
Wind sighs through
The trees sending a chill
Over the water.
I hold close my coat and
Head up the path,
Trembling with this secret vision.

Larry Ellingson *Fiction*

Blackbird

He had been home about a month when he found the letter. He recognized the pale blue envelope first, with its red and blue border, then the word FREE in his own scrawl instead of postage. It had been read and then left in a pile of junk mail and old bills. He felt a queer numbness when he read what he had written. When he finished, he went back and read it again slowly.

Dear Mom and Dad,

I am writing this from a hospital in Da Nang. I'm OK, just some shrapnel in my left leg. The doctor says I'll be fine. We were on patrol near Quang Tri when we were pinned down in a rice paddy. Smitty was killed. He got hit first, they sniped at us first and Smitty was shot. Ski got killed too, and Holman lost both legs. Holman had the radio and that's why we didn't get back-up sooner. I'm the only one left now out of my original squad. I'm so short now that they won't send me back to the bush. Expect to be heading home soon so don't send any more letters.

Love,

Rick

Rick carefully folded the letter and replaced it in the stack. He needed to get out. He grabbed the rifle as he headed out the door. It was October, Indian summer with warm, bright days sending up the roasted, tannic odor of dead leaves, good squirrel hunting days. Rick stepped carefully over the rows of corn stubble, walking toward the tree line. The .22 felt awkward in his hands, so small and light. A blackbird flushed near him, squawking as it flew to the top of a distant tree. He felt a rush of adrenalin.

"Goddam bird," Rick said.

"You short-timers sure get nervous," Smitty teased.

"Fuckin-eh, you would too."

"Not me. I don't give a shit. That's the trick, if you don't give a shit you'll be OK. It's nervous bastards like you that need to worry."

"I felt the same way once, and did the same crazy things you're doing now. Standing up in a firefight and unloading a full clip. Volunteering to walk point. Acting like some kind of goddamn hero because making it this far must mean you're invincible."

Smitty was quiet, like he hadn't heard. "Maybe I'll go to Bangkok for R & R," he said. "Ski had a great time there, got drunk and laid every night."

"Why don't you go to Tokyo?" Rick said. "See some sights, buy a stereo. You can get a great stereo for half what you'd pay back home."

Smitty grinned his wise-ass grin. "Do I look like a fuckin' tourist?"

They walked along in silence, kicking up powdery dust that settled over the staggered column of marines and coated them a ghostlike gray.

"Y'know," Rick said, "it's a damn shame the old squad didn't take R & R together. We planned to, didn't we? And then Incenzo got killed and after that Guitterez got fucked up. Ski was lucky that time, the time Guitterez got hit, cause Ski was point man and must have stepped right over the mine and then Guitterez stepped right on the son-of-a-bitch. That's when Ski went to the lieutenant and said he had to have R & R and so he went by himself . . . so there it is."

"There it is," Smitty agreed.

It was late afternoon when the column was halted. The tree line shaded a small village about 300 meters ahead. The marines strung out across the rice paddies and slowly advanced, picking their way cautiously along the dikes, sidestepping suspicious rocks or clumps of grass. It was useless though; there were so many ways that the V.C. could hide a mine. Thick, muggy air rose from the paddies. The men sweated heavily under their flak jackets and helmets and they held their M-16s with both hands.

It started with sniper fire, a few sporadic shots that sent them for cover. Squad leaders signaled to fan out. Some got up and ran, splashing through the paddies to dive behind a dike. Smitty jumped up too and ran, firing bursts and, as he was shot, he leaped and spread his arms like he was trying to get airborne, and then he fell face down in the brown water. Holman was trying to get the radio to the lieutenant. He made short, crouching runs, diving into the muddy water and cursing each time he landed. He waited until they were shooting at someone else and then ran, hunched over, zigzagging, making good time, and then the ground erupted, lifting his torso as his legs blew away. Small arms fire kept them down, and then the mortars came, exploding randomly on the neatly patterned landscape like violent, savage moves on a game board. Rick pushed his face into the mud, trying to sink into the earth. The ground was pounding, each blast closer and louder until it became a single roar, and he felt big clods of mud spatter him. Deafened, he looked to his left where the close one had landed and saw Ski holding his neck and staring at the empty sky. He wanted to go to him, but his body wouldn't move; he was part of the soil, a lump of clay. His squad was gone now; he was the last one.

The company was pinned down all night. Mortars came in just often enough to keep them from rest, and the wounded moaned and cried out. At dawn they moved into the village. The V.C. were gone by then and old women and children were all that they found. The marines herded the villagers together and set fire to their huts and their rice and they threw grenades into the tunnels beneath their huts. Choppers flew in to pick up the badly wounded first, and then the other wounded and then the dead.

Rick limped past the row of body bags, past the burning huts and through the smoke. At the edge of the village, high on a treetop, he saw the blackbird. Mechanically he took aim, let out his breath and gently squeezed the trigger.

The bird tumbled through the bare branches of the oak and landed at his feet. It lay fluttering on the ground, pumping scarlet blood on black feathers. Finally, it lay still. He began to shake, and the rifle dropped from his hands. He moved heavily toward the creek. In a clearing surrounded by tall oaks he crawled into a shallow hole that was lined with matted yellow grass. In times past it had been a house, a fort and a foxhole. Now it was a cradle, and the Earth rocked him as he wept.

Time

Everything fell off the edge of my bed tonight
into the dimscape of my bedroom
time was one of those things for me
though it kept running down your fingers
strip me please
I want that place on your chest in the center of my
bed I want my burns to stop aching to stop
being rubbed by time
I'm not used to not being the fire but I've never
been burned before so I thought it was you
that I was the one playing with it but
I think the fire is here in the middle
with me avoiding time and you doing . . . whatever the
hell it is that you think you do
to me

Everything fell off the edge of my bed tonight
into the dimscape of my bedroom
we floated as skin and human
me against your chest sweating and burning
all consumed and I wonder if you heard it
if you felt it if your heart pounded
as hard as mine if time slipped like it did
for me or if it was just my bones you felt
under my skin
just bones and wet flesh just you enjoying
my reaction to you

Everything fell off the edge of my bed tonight
into the dimscape of my bedroom
I feel the words that are in me
I can hear them like a song I haven't
yet met (that I already know by heart)
but your fingers—painting time over the arch
of me—steal my words and they are smoke
featureless and drifting off the edge of my bed
along with everything else and anything that
ever mattered to me fair enough
I would have only asked
for more

Everything fell off the edge of my bed tonight
into the dimscape of my bedroom

Dennis Herschbach *Poetry*

Beyond Repair

Broken stands in the kitchen,
spoons leftovers into a bowl.
Sounds of hate ring from stainless,
slicing the damning silence.

She looks up—glares through narrowed
  eyes;
fracturing words spill out:
over! had it!
no more!

Broken sits at a table, head bowed,
expression gone from a weathered face,
a cup of untouched coffee, unnoticed,
cools near his elbow.

Hands—beaten, gnarled,
pick calluses and scars—
useless hands, unemployed,
hands battered as his spirit.

He looks up;
words form on his lips,
die before they are born,
and his throat cramps.

Broken—what happens
when love dies,
truth becomes lies,
memories are empty echoes.

Shards, too scattered to be
  found,
cannot be fitted together,
will never be whole; there's
  not
enough glue left in their
  bucket.

Luke Anderson *Fiction*

Incident at First and Main

Weekdays, about 10 a.m., the "G'old Boys" gather around the table in Arthur's Cafe to roll dice for coffee, embellish old stories and, most importantly, hear the latest breaking news in the tiny village of Brookton. The "Boys" know all what's happening because their ace reporters are Peter and Harold. Peter's beat is First Lutheran where he is the janitor, and Harold, a.k.a. *Brookton Herald*, is a regular at Elroy's Tap.

While hurrying to Arthur's one twenty-below morning, Peter and Harold peered through peep-holes in frosted car windows and collided at First Street and Main Avenue.

The incident went unreported.

Betty J. Benner *Creative Nonfiction*

Spiral

We sat elbow to elbow, some on the floor, some on chairs, with wine and pinwheel sandwiches, listening to poems inspired by photos taken by local people. Poetography, they called it. These were the contest winners.

I wanted to get to the bottom of it.

I fingered the spiral necklace I always wear, waiting for the English teacher to read her verse. (Hers was third from the last of the thirty poems; my sandwich was crumbs and it was almost nine o'clock.) Her poem spoke of the spirals in nature and how we copy them in our lives, in our architecture—in her photo, this staircase in the Vatican, for example, dwindles down to blackness.

I wanted to get to the bottom of it.

To understand why something in me is drawn to spirals. My necklace, for instance; the flowerpot on my sill, shell-shaped, the spiraling lines complimenting the rough clay; the rubber stamp I sometimes use on notepaper; my recognition of the spirals in pine cones, clockwise and counterclockwise; my remembering without consciously memorizing a stanza from "The Chambered Nautilus."

Tonight the poet speaks of Fibonacci's Sequence. She explains for me when I approach her later in the crowd how the spiral has everything to do with mathematics. I am not mathematically inclined; tenth grade geometry was stretching it.

But I wanted to get to the bottom of it.

I am not the only one excited by spirals. First, a thirteenth century Italian, and now . . . She was animated, this soft-spoken young woman. She reached for my spiral notebook and with assurance listed the Fibonacci Sequence, a series of numbers beginning with 0 and 1. Use the simple rule, she said: add the last two numbers to get the next, and one goes on into infinity. She showed me too how this sequence turns into a spiral when you pile Fibonacci-measured squares on top of one another and connect the corners. It's all right there in my little notebook.

I didn't get to the bottom of it. Perhaps that's the beauty of spirals. They are a part of the magic of the universe and just keep on going whether I understand them or not.

But wait . . . maybe I did, sort of, bottom out. Maybe recognizing the infinity of spirals puts new meaning to leaving one's low-vaulted past for a dome more vast till I at last am free.

Kristin F. Johnson *Poetry Honorable Mention*

The Morning After

the wine bottles lay
on the blue nightstand like they,
too, were hung over.

Apologia

My sincerest apologies: please forgive my listlessness
when action was required. I feel small and insignificant.

It's human to sometimes act inhuman. So if I offered hope
with my words, rest assured the gesture was accidental.

My sincerest apologies: but love and mistakes are what we
make together. There are countless ways to come undone,

some more exquisite than others and, by my very nature,
I gravitate towards the unglamorous options. Excuse my

voracity, my pomade-slick intentions, the mangled lyrics
of my broken soul in stereo. My sincerest apologies:

I never intended to waterboard your heart, or strong-arm
you into divulging all of your awful secrets, even those

you didn't know you had. My sincerest apologies:
the equations are familiar, yet impossible to solve—

a whole man alongside a fraction of a woman
try to fashion a relationship with the remainder

of what divides them. The missing variables cause love
to slide downward from the weight of expectations

like an overburdened refrigerator magnet. The derivative
is a world filled with couples who never resolve their issues,

wedged in precarious arrangements that work, for now.
My sincerest apologies: I probably screwed up, but love

has a thousand-page operator's manual which I failed to open.
It's impossible to follow instructions that I never read.

Kari E. Hagstrom *Poetry*

Trajectory

Maybe
Maybe our lives
Are like sub-atomic particles
Set in motion eons ago,
Just particles in motion
Set on a collision
Course so long ago,
So far away,
Galaxies and universes away,
That we can't even begin to
Gain any perspective.
Particles in an atomic collider
Set in motion
Colliding, exploding, accelerating
Each other through synchronicities,
Humble little events,
Hardly even noticeable,
As invisible as quarks
And electrons, changing
Trajectories
Of galaxies,
Of universes.

"The talking stick is a Native American tradition used to facilitate an orderly discussion. The stick is made of wood, decorated with feathers or fur, beads or paint, or a combination of all. Usually speakers are arranged in a talking circle and the stick is passed from hand to hand as the discussion progresses. It encourages all to speak and allows each person to speak without interruption. The talking stick brings all natural elements together to guide and direct the talking circle." —Anne Dunn

This year, we received 334 submissions
from 164 writers. The editorial board selected
87 poems, 29 creative nonfiction,
and 25 fiction pieces from 99 writers
for inclusion in this volume. Please submit again!

www.thetalkingstick.com
www.jackpinewriters.com

CONTRIBUTORS 2012

(Without the following contributors, this Talking Stick would not have been possible! Thank you to everyone!)

Friends/Single

Bev Erickson

Sandra Larson

Good Friends/Single

Sonja Kosler

Margaret M. Marty

Susan McMillan

Vince O'Connor

Bob Sullivan

Friends/Couple

Patricia and Don Conner

Scott and Jessica Stewart

Willis Enterprises

(Beagle Books & Sister Wolf Books)

Special Friends/Single

Sandra Clough

Mike Lein

Sharon Spartz

Benefactors

Louise Bottrell

Charmaine Pappas Donovan

Jerry Mevissen

Harlan and Marlene Stoehr

Author List

Luke Anderson
Robert K. Anderson
Lina Belar
Betty J. Benner
James Bettendorf
Scott Daniel Boras
Nicole Borg
Louise Bottrell
Beth Diane Bradley
Kirstin Ruth Bratt
Tim J. Brennan
Eric Chandler
Sharon Chmielarz
Chet Corey
Joanne Cress
Sue Reed Crouse
Frances Ann Crowley
Sharon K. Donohue
Charmaine Pappas Donovan
Barbara Draper
Neil Dyer
Larry Ellingson
Jeanne Everhart
Laurie Fabrizio
Katie Fish
Michael Forbes
Cindy Fox
David Francis
Katie Gilbertson
Flo Golod
Georgia A. Greeley
Marlys Guimaraes
Kari E. Hagstrom

Kate Halverson
Helen Hansen
Laura L. Hansen
Sharon Harris
Audrey Kletscher Helbling
Heidi Hemmer
Dennis Herschbach
Catherine Holm
Christine Madeline Holm
Marion C. Holtey
Rhoda Jackson
Kristin F. Johnson
Linda M. Johnson
George H. Johnston IV
Miriam Kagol
Sangita Kalarickal
Ryan W. Keller
Danny Klecko
Kathryn Knudson
Sonja Kosler
Rebecca J. Krystosek
Jamee Larson
Mike Lein
Renee Loehr
Sister Kate Martin
Margaret M. Marty
Marianne McNamara
Kathryn Kirmis Medellin
Jerry Mevissen
Michael Kiesow Moore
Joanne Moren
Marsh Muirhead
Laura K. Murray

Deb Nelson
Kelly Nelson
Ronald J. Palmer
Mike C. Paulus
Lucelia Pazar
Susan Perala-Dewey
Deanna Perchyshyn
Niomi Rohn Phillips
Shasha C. Porter
Adrian S. Potter
Kit Rohrbach
Jim Russell
Larry Schug
Richard Fenton Sederstrom
Sheri Smith
Susan Kathleen Spindler
Thomas C. Stetzler
Scott Stewart
Marlene Mattila Stoehr
Bob Sullivan
Sharon Tauber
David J. Thoelke
John Thornberg
Peggy Trojan
Susan Niemela Vollmer
Justin Watkins
Bonnie West
Mary Scully Whitaker
LuAnne White
Cheryl Weibye Wilke
Marilyn Wolff
Tarah L. Wolff
Kevin Zepper